TABLE OF CONTENTS

I0569485

Part One

Part Two

PART ONE

DEBORA RESNICK

THE LANGUAGE PROFESSOR

KS
Kravitz & Sons
INNOVATORS IN PUBLISHING, MARKETING AND ADVERTISING

Kravitz and Sons LLC
204 E Arlington Blvd. Suite B
Greenville, NC 27858

Published by Kravitz and Sons LLC.

ISBN: 979-8-89639-702-1 (sc)
ISBN: 979-8-89639-701-4 (e)

CHAPTER 1

The bastard, the fucking bastard, Naomi swore as she searched frantically for the memo granting her a one year leave of absence. Eugene couldn't do what he was doing, he couldn't.

Ah, here was the memo. Naomi read it through quickly. Oh god, Eugene had every right to do what he was doing.

Naomi read the memo through a second time. God, how could she have been so stupid?

The Steering Committee has approved your request for a one-year leave of absence commencing August 1, 198-.

(A) During this time your seniority and experience will not accumulate.

(B) This Leave of Absence does not guarantee you the same position upon your return.

(C) This Leave of Absence does guarantee you a professional position upon your return.

That second point was as clear as could be, how could she have missed it, yet she had missed it, Naomi thought. She was totally screwed.

Naomi raced back to Danielle's study and handed Danielle the memo. "I'm afraid Eugene can do what he is doing. Take a look at this."

Danielle read the memo and looked up. "Is this what you understood when you accepted this condition?"

"Of course not," Naomi replied. "The then Director of Human Resources who wrote the memo, Jim Palmer, was from a college that had joined an admissions consortium run by the French colleges. The winter before I went on leave there had been talk at Penfield of joining the consortium. Joining that consortium would have significantly changed the way the Admissions Office functioned. Jim inserted that clause to protect Penfield."

"But Penfield has not joined the consortium?"

"No."

"What does your union contract say?"

"I didn't look at our union contract. I'm not even sure I have a copy of it at home. Just a minute."

Naomi raced back to look through her papers.

The fucking bastard, Naomi continued to swear. She knew exactly why Eugene was doing this, because she had balked at admitting the son of an acquaintance of his the year before she went on leave. But go prove it, and in what court of law?

Ah, thank god, here was her union contract.

A professional who is granted a leave of absence without pay may continue to benefit from group insurance…

No, that was not what she was looking for.

A professional who has been granted a leave of absence without pay shall resume his position on the date agreed to at the time of his leave.

Naomi felt the pounding of her heart ease up a little. She walked back to Danielle's study. "The union contract seems pretty clear," she said, "here, read this."

Danielle read the clause and looked up. "I'm sure it's the union contract that counts. There's nothing in the memo that says that the contract is being suspended."

"Maybe there's something about that in the contract too." Naomi took back the contract and re- skimmed the article about leaves of absence. There was nothing in the first clause. Her heart began pounding again. There was nothing in the second clause.

Any special agreement…

The pounding eased up again, this was what she was looking for.

Any special agreement between a professional and the college is null and void and cannot change the provisions of this contract nor add to it nor diminish it in any way whatsoever. "Take a look at this." Naomi handed Danielle the contract.

Danielle read it and looked up. "Well, that's as clear as can be. If Penfield argues that this was a special agreement - which it wasn't, of course – then it's still not allowed, assuming for one moment that you ever assented to the interpretation Eugene is putting on the memo."

"I'm willing to bet that that's not what happened at all. The thought of being bound by a union contract would never have entered Eugene's mind," Naomi said. "What happened is that Eugene snapped his fingers last week, two weeks ago, who knows when, and everyone in his entourage jumped.

"The stupidest thing," Naomi continued, "is that I got a discretionary pay increase while I was away. Six months ago Eugene tells me that I'm terrific and now he takes my job away. It makes no sense at all. But then I don't think Eugene cares whether it makes sense or not as long as people jump."

"I think you should call your union representative," Danielle said.

"If I can find someone, they're probably all away on holiday." Naomi looked at her watch. "It's too late now, I'll call first thing in the morning." She began to flip through the pages of the union contract. "You know, there are ways the College can move people around, the College does have the right to make organizational changes, to make changes to the services it offers."

"All right, let's assume that that's what they wanted to do," Danielle said.

Naomi turned to the article on Organizational Change. She began reading and looked up moments later. "There's only this." She passed the document to Danielle.

Any transfer resulting from the enforcement of a reorganization plan is obligatory for the professional concerned...

"No, that does not give Eugene the right to do what he is doing," Danielle said. "You told me that when you spoke to Reuben he said that your position was being posted. If the posting is identical to your job description, then they can't argue that there has been any organizational change. If they wanted to proceed according to this article, they would have had to reorganize something, change something, but they haven't done anything of the kind."

"But there's nothing to stop them from doing that now."

"True. But even if they legitimately wanted to get you out of admissions, I don't see how they could do that and still have an admissions office. They could add responsibilities, that is, change your job description even significantly, but eliminate the position completely, it's impossible, even though they're not even pretending that's what they're doing because they're posting your job."

"It is possible to eliminate positions justifiably," Naomi persisted, and she flipped to the article on Surplus of Personnel and scanned it quickly. "No, none of these conditions apply," she said a moment later. "There has been no decrease of students and Penfield has neither amalgamated nor merged services with another college, which would have been the case had we joined that consortium."

"They can't do it, Darling, they just can't do it."

"There's one more thing. Surely, the College can make changes to a job description, to the duties they have assigned to an employee." Naomi flipped to the article on Employment Security. "Ah, here's something."

The college shall not force any professional to accept a transfer...

"Exactly," Danielle said. "That's consistent with the previous article. Unless there has been a formal re-organization of services, which there hasn't been, the College can't force you to change jobs."

"Right. Oh, and here," Naomi said, "there's more."

This article shall apply to any professional declared surplus...

Whenever a professional position becomes vacant in the college, any professional who has been declared surplus shall automatically be an eligible candidate for that position.

"In other words," Naomi summarized what they had just read, "even if they declare me surplus, which they cannot, they have to hire me back for the job they are kicking me out of. It's in the same category – it's the same job, for crying out loud."

"Are they stupid, Naomi, or what?"

"No, not stupid," Naomi explained. "You have to understand that you're talking about Eugene Guzman. Even if Reuben knew his union contract, which I am not sure is the case, and had tried to explain it to Eugene, Eugene would not have listened. The man doesn't listen to anyone, he is above the law, he is the law as far as he is concerned."

"Well, he may think he is above the law, but according to the union contract, it is impossible for him to do what he is doing."

"Yet he is doing it."

"All I can say is that it is disgraceful that this is happening, and in the public sector too."

"It's all because of Tom Garner, you remember, I told you about him."

"So you didn't think he should have been admitted, big deal. You're terrific at what you do, you work hard, you're very responsible, you're a great organizer –"

"That's the problem, that I am competent. Eugene does not like competent people, he especially does not like competent women, I'm certain of that, but go prove it."

"There are several things you have to ask your union representative, whether you should apply for the job when it is posted, whether you should file a grievance immediately or whether you should wait –"

"I expect I have to wait for the posting, for the offence to be committed."

"You have to ask."

"I guess it will also be important what the posting looks like, whether it is identical to my job description or not."

"I think you should call Reuben and ask for a confirmation in writing of all that he said to you on the telephone."

"I did. He said he would send me something."

"And now there is nothing else to do. Do you think you can try not to think about this for a little while?"

"I can try but I doubt that I'll succeed."

CHAPTER 2

Her and Danielle's reading of the union contract was correct, Naomi thought.

It was correct. If she were on her own she might not be so sure, but she had confidence in Danielle, Eugene could not do what he was doing.

Couldn't – but what did that mean since he sure as hell was doing it?

Couldn't in the sense that he had no right to do it, that what he was doing went directly counter to her contract. Her leave-of-absence memo did not stand alone, words from it could not be removed and toyed with at will, the memo had to be understood in context.

And the context was clear.

Or at least it seemed to be.

No, it was clear, she and Danielle were right, Eugene had no right to do what he was doing.

CHAPTER 3

There was nobody in the Union office, Naomi thought. She would have to wait until Monday morning to speak to someone there.

In the meantime all she could do was run through her arguments again.

And again.

She hated this, this forced scrutinizing of words the meaning of which had been perfectly clear a year ago, which suddenly had a new and damning meaning applied to them that could be offset only by laborious explanation.

Yes, that second sentence in the memo said that she was not guaranteed her position upon her return, it said so plainly and clearly. But her union contract said that when a person went on leave, that person resumed her position upon returning from her leave. The union contract also laid out the conditions under which she might not resume her position – none of which applied.

That same contract also stated that no one, neither employer nor employee, could annul or subvert any clauses of the contract. So while her reading of the memo was consistent with the union contract – it allowed the employer to make changes to her job if the nature of her job changed - the employer's – in this instance Eugene's - reading of the memo subverted the union contract completely since, unless there was a change to her job, she was guaranteed her job upon her return.

She just hoped that the posting would not be too different from her job description.

And she wouldn't know this until Saturday.

CHAPTER 4

It was identical, Naomi breathed with relief after she finished reading the job posting, not one word of the job description was different from her original job description.

That was one less battle to fight, to prove that a small wording change had not changed the nature of her job.

Yes, this was the character of the fray she had been thrown into, to prove that words meant what they meant, all words, not just a few words extracted in isolation from the memo, that the memo itself did not stand alone and that behind it lay a larger logic that had to be obeyed.

The fucking bastard.

CHAPTER 5

"You know what this means, Naomi, don't you," Lynne brought her fist down on the table, "Eugene is saying that competence does not count. Well, by golly, we're going to show him that it does. And we're going to get you your job back, I promise you."

Tears sprang to Naomi's eyes. "Thanks, Lynne. I -" Naomi took a tissue out of her purse and wiped her eyes. "I'm just so teary these days," Naomi wiped her eyes again and blew her nose. "Kindness always makes me cry," she gulped, "and you're being -" She could not continue.

"It's as if Eugene were doing this to me, Naomi," Lynne said softly, "or to Charles."

Naomi nodded her head in acknowledgement. She knew that if she tried to speak, she would start to sob uncontrollably.

"Now here's what we are going to do," Lynne said.

. . . .

Everything Lynne proposed was good and right, Naomi thought as she drove home from lunch, but rather than remove the fear from her belly, Lynne's proposals had intensified it. Because what Lynne proposed was nothing less than all-out-war, with Naomi's person being the zone in which the war was to be fought.

Naomi was to follow the advice of the union lawyers whom she had finally reached in the morning and formally apply for her position.

As well, their local union was to file grievances immediately against the posting.

None of that aroused fear. The public manifesto did – it was a brilliant idea, of course, to write a letter warning Penfield employees away from applying for her job. But the fear came from the nature of the manifesto – they were going to put one in every employee's mail box – from this open acceptance of hostilities – what nefarious means would Eugene now find with which to punish her – and, last but not least, from placing herself in the public eye – she hated being the centre of attention, being talked about, having the merits of her case discussed by people to whom her case would be but a passing news item while her whole being had come under attack.

They were also to send a letter to the Human Rights Commission complaining about Eugene's treatment of women at Penfield. When Eugene got wind of that, what would he do in retaliation?

But she had accepted Lynne's strategy. She had the utmost confidence in Lynne, just as she had in Danielle. Left to her own devices she would have done the first two things only, applied for her job and filed a grievance. Then she would have sat in her corner and waited as her case wound its way through the union's legal instances. She would never have thought of issuing a manifesto or of writing the Human Rights Commission. But Lynne knew Eugene because she had been at Penfield longer than Naomi and because Charles, her husband, was Vice-President of Administrative Services at Penfield and worked under Eugene. Eugene had been bullying Charles and the few administrators left from the preceding administration for years, the bullying had now been extended to their ranks, that of the Professionals, and Lynne was not going to sit back and let that happen.

It was interesting how she and Lynne had become friends. Lynne worked in Student Services, an area which did not interact much with Admissions. Also, Student Services was located in a building to which Naomi did not have much occasion to go. But one day during the fall - she would have been too busy in the spring to stay behind and chat with anyone – she had gone to Student Services for a meeting and after the meeting had ended up staying on in Lynne's office. Lynne's background was interesting – she had originally trained as a nurse but had changed direction and had just finished her university degree by going to school at night. They had talked about that and the next thing Naomi knew, she was telling Lynne about something she hadn't even realized had been on her mind.

Naomi's predecessor in Admissions, Jane, had been the first incumbent in the job. It was she who had created all the structures and procedures Naomi had inherited and who had hired the staff Naomi had inherited. This chat with Lynne took place about two years after Naomi had been in the job, and all that time she had been wondering what her assistants thought of her, what the faculty with whom she came into contact thought of her, whether she was measuring up to the big shoes of her predecessor, except she had never been conscious of doing so, it was while talking to Lynne that she had first put her concern into words.

It was nothing that Lynne had said, it was the quality of Lynne's attentiveness that had elicited this confession from her. When she left Lynne's office she had been amazed – Jane's ghost, which had been hovering over her since she had been on the job, had disappeared. She realized immediately that she had met someone extraordinary and that she wanted to be friends with her.

The next step had been to tell Lynne that she was gay.

Telling people she was gay was not a problem for her – Danielle was much more wary than she was and frowned on her openness. Telling people that her girls lived with their father was another matter. There had been good reason for this. She had agreed to live an Orthodox Jewish life when she had married Josh but had not been willing to do so when she had left, and taking Tara and Ruth with her would have meant uprooting them completely. When talking about her gayness, she couldn't help talking about her girls, and while she knew she had done the right thing by them, she knew that most people would frown on her behavior.

Lynne's response had been perfect. "Thank you for sharing this most important part of your life with me," she had said, and their friendship had been sealed.

How could she not follow Lynne's advice *in toto*, how could she not put her faith in a friend whose judgment she trusted and admired, whose knowledge of Penfield was profound and whose heart was as vast as her courage?

She could not and would not.

CHAPTER 6

She hated this, Naomi thought, hated it, hated it, hated it.
She crossed out the word *great*, reluctance was sufficient. She reread the last sentence. *I submit this application with reluctance and under protest, as I feel* – she crossed out the word *feel* and replaced it with the word *consider* – *consider the position of Coordinator of Admissions to be rightfully* – she crossed out the word *rightfully,* thought about it for a moment and then put it back - *mine.*

Oh, she almost forgot. She inserted the words *Without Prejudice* at the top of the letter.

She skimmed through the letter again. All the relevant points were there, the list of the job's qualifications, the list of her evaluations – there were six *exceeds the job requirements* and six *fully meets the job requirements,* contributed equally by Derek, her first supervisor, and Reuben, her second supervisor. And, of course, there was the evaluation granting her a discretionary pay increase for which Reuben had recommended her and that officially recognized *"…her mastery of the knowledge associated with her field, the excellence with which she accomplished the most complex tasks, and the noticeable leadership she exercised while carrying out her duties."*

No, there was not one extraneous word, not a drop of the outrage she felt that she should have to write this letter, that this was happening. Competence did not count, Lynne had said. Worse from her viewpoint was that words had stopped counting. For Eugene had approved that discretionary pay increase while she had been on leave – she realized now that Eugene must have done so because he had tapped Reuben to replace Jim Palmer who had resigned and this had been a way of throwing Reuben a sop, but Eugene had approved it. If words did not count, however, what was the use of pointing this out, of enumerating her excellent evaluations, of proving – that's it, there was no proving anything, because words had been emptied of their meaning.

And that's what was so terrible, that she had to go through the motions – it had taken a lot of effort to pare her letter down to what it was now, to cut away all the detail she had initially included demonstrating how much the job entailed and how well she knew it, but what purpose would that have served? Her words, whether more or less comprehensive, would not convince, her cause, no matter how just, would not make Eugene relent. She had worked and worked and had known as she worked that she was wasting her time.

CHAPTER 7

BLACKLISTED

*The Position of
Coordinator of Admissions
at
Penfield College*

*O*n August 1, 198-, Naomi Singer was granted a one-year leave of absence from her position of Coordinator of Admissions at Penfield College to study French in France.

Nine days before resuming her position, Naomi was informed by the Director of Human Resources that the position was no longer hers and that it was being posted.

The Association of Penfield College Professionals maintains that the position of Coordinator of Admissions is not vacant, that Naomi Singer is the legitimate incumbent of this position, and calls upon faculty and staff to boycott the hiring process and to refrain from applying for this position.

We will keep the College community informed of further developments in this case.

*Andrew Roper, President
Association of Penfield College Professionals*

There it was, Naomi thought as she held the notice in her hand, her open declaration of war, her public taking up of the gauntlet Eugene had thrown down and the acceptance of his challenge.

She could feel the fear snaking through her body. What would Eugene do now?

That was the worst of it, trying to understand the man's thoughts, trying to anticipate the man's deeds, because the world she had known had changed, Eugene had removed all the signposts, he had shaken the very foundations of her existence.

What kind of man did what he was doing?

She had been naïve, foolish and naïve, and what was worse, she had been amply warned, but she had not read the warnings. For shortly after she had arrived at Penfield there had been the John Jamieson affair. John had been one of the original administrators at Penfield but had run afoul of Eugene about six months after Eugene had been appointed President and had been summarily fired. The entire administrative corps except for Hannah Weir, the Academic Dean, had taken up John's cause, but to no avail. The issue had been brought to Penfield's Board of Directors but the dismissal had been upheld. This had lead to a wholesale exodus of administrators, including Derek, the man who had hired her and who – it was only later that she realized it - had acted as a buffer between her and anyone who tried to put undue pressure on the Admissions Office.

The second warning came a few days before Derek's resignation was to take effect, when Naomi received a call from Hannah Weir asking her to review the application of a certain Jimmy Renaldo, a call she would never have received if Derek had not been on his way out. "Jimmy barely passed high school. We've refused hundreds of students stronger than Jimmy," she had said to Hannah. "I'd like you to reevaluate his file," Hannah had said. "I've looked at it, Hannah, there's nothing extenuating there," she had replied. "Naomi, I want you to look at it again," Hannah had insisted. And that was when she had gone too far, "Who is Jimmy Rinaldo anyway?" she had asked. And she had been treated to a heated lecture about respecting authority and about remembering that the position of Coordinator of Admissions derived from that of the Dean. After Hannah had finished, Naomi had agreed to admit Jimmy Rinaldo. She gave her staff their instructions, left her office and walked over to the nearby park to try to recuperate.

She felt as if she had been bludgeoned. What had that been about? But slowly it had begun to make sense. She had heard that Eugene was playing games with the budget, that he was insisting there was a shortfall of students. Jimmy Rinaldo was probably the President's friend, then, not Hannah's. That would explain why Hannah had been so upset with her, she was upset with herself too, no doubt. And for her to have asked 'Who is Jimmy Rinaldo?' was to have breached the rules, was to have said openly that influence was at play here rather than merit. But if that's the way things were, why pretend otherwise?

A year later, when Reuben, who had replaced Derek as Registrar, had come to her and asked her to review Tom Garner's file, she had still not wised up and she had told him it was impossible. "But the President wants him in," Reuben had said. "Tell the President what I just said, that we have refused dozens of students stronger than Tom." Reuben had come back two more times to talk to her about Tom, and the last time he hadn't asked, he had told her, admit Tom Garner.

And now she was paying for her incredible naïveté, for her incredible obliviousness.

Although, again, what kind of man was Eugene who, instead of giving her a talking-to the way Hannah had done, had pulled out all the stops, had repaid a small slight to his authority with a savagery, an implacability, she found incomprehensible.

BLACKLISTED
The Position of...

On August 1, 198-, Naomi Singer was granted a one-year leave of absence from her...

It read well, Naomi thought. There was not one word too many, just as there had not been in her application letter. She had pared everything down to the bone again, hard as that had been, but the results had been worth it – the manifesto was stark but incontrovertible.

But it did leave her feeling terribly exposed. And terrified.

CHAPTER 8

"What happened?" Harold asked, commiseration in his voice, the *Blacklisted* notice in his hand.

"The notice says it all," Naomi replied. Harold was a junior administrator at Penfield and she and Harold had a pleasant professional relationship, but if Harold thought for one second that she would confide in him, that she would tell him anything that he could carry back to Reuben, with whom he was friends, he was mistaken.

After a few minutes Harold got up to leave. "If I can do anything to help..." he said.

"Thanks, Harold." Naomi said. Not on your life, Harold, she thought. Since Reuben's phone call, the world had suddenly become composed of us and them, and the number of us people had become very, very small.

CHAPTER 9

Naomi read through the union grievance again. She was telling her story for a third time and from yet a different angle. And there was no room for feelings here, just as there had not been in her application letter or the manifesto. What was interesting, however, was that in writing up the grievance – writing taught you, she had long ago realized, the process of having to put your thoughts onto paper refined them, sometimes even changed them - she had discovered yet another misdemeanor on the part of the College, one that gave even more force to her argument, not that she needed it.

The union contract enumerated various categories of professional positions, admissions officer, academic advisor, librarian, psychologist. It also listed the responsibilities and qualifications of each position and described the formal process that had to be followed when hiring a professional. Her present position, which consisted of 'certain duties' in the Dean's office, was not listed as one of these categories. Neither had her responsibilities ever been defined, nor had there ever been a formal hiring process. On all three counts, then, 'certain duties' did not constitute a professional position.

The seemingly damning, second condition in the memo – that she had not been guaranteed the same position upon her return – had been undone by the third condition – that she had been guaranteed a professional position upon her return. As this guarantee had not been fulfilled, this further upheld her contention that, her position having been unchanged, the College had guaranteed her position upon her return.

But a lot of good this additional argument would do, Naomi thought, although there was great satisfaction in having come up with it and having presented it in a concise manner.

CHAPTER 10

She should not have gone to the grievance hearing, Naomi thought, it had been a terrible mistake. It was one thing to think about the injustice being done to her, it was another to watch Reuben stonewall his way through the hearing, to have no response to her arguments, to hear him recite that second sentence in the memo over and over again even though she had demolished its strength, even though she had demonstrated the College's bad faith by quoting the third sentence of the memo back to him.

She had wanted to scream, to grab Reuben by his jacket lapels and shake him. She had especially wanted to wipe that smug smile of his face.

Reuben the brash, Reuben the ambitious -

Clearly, going along with Eugene's wickedness had not caused Reuben to lose any sleep, nothing caused Reuben to lose any sleep, he was so imbued with the sense of his own importance...

She hated Reuben, she hated Eugene, she hated them, hated them, hated them.

CHAPTER 11

No, she did not hate Reuben and Eugene, Naomi thought, she just did not understand them.

What motivated a Eugene – Reuben was easy, he had happened to be in Human Resources when Eugene decided to strike and had had to go along with Eugene's machinations despite the absence of any grounds for doing so – but she would never understand a Eugene, never understand firing, or trying to fire, an excellent employee –

It was as Lynne had said, competence did not count.

But then what did count, only personal power, obedience? Where was principle, where was competence, where was striving for excellence?

She had had one encounter with Eugene since she had been back, on her second day at work, when Eugene had inadvertently wandered into the Dean's outer office. "Look who's back," he had remarked flippantly. "Yes," she had replied easily, conversationally. And, she had added, she had spent a very productive year in France. Eugene had not answered but had turned on his heel and left.

So, the man did not do small talk, Naomi had thought, he did not do normal, everyday conversation.

A week later she had seen Eugene with Lynne's husband, Charles. The two men had happened to meet in the hall and she had heard Charles ask Eugene whether Eugene had made a decision yet about a certain contract. Eugene had not slowed his pace but had kept on walking, forcing Charles to follow from behind. From Charles' expression she could tell that he had not gotten an answer. Eugene was heading for his office, where, once inside, the discussion would be over, and she had heard Charles try one last time to get Eugene to commit himself, "So I'll call Caron, theirs is the best overall coverage," Charles had said. Eugene had grimaced, wisecracked, but ultimately had left the matter hanging.

Charles had two alternatives then, to go ahead and, if that did not turn out well, to be crucified, or not to go ahead and, if that did not turn out well, to be crucified. The point of the exercise was not to get things done, then, it was to keep people off balance, to set them up, to dangle them on a string in order to have the power to cut the string or not.

She did not understand this manner of running things, this manner of dealing with people, she simply did not understand.

CHAPTER 12

"I blew it, Lynne, I blew it."

"Easy, Naomi, easy. Tell me exactly what happened."

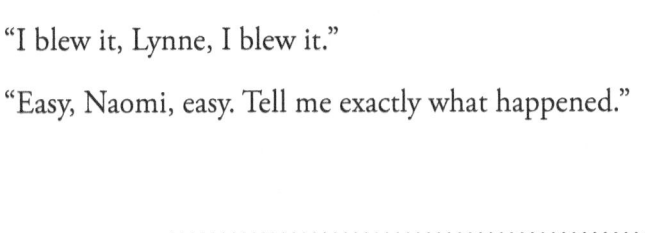

Lynne was kind, Lynne absolved her of all fault, but she knew, Naomi thought, she had lost it, she had done what she had promised herself she would not do during the interview, lose her temper, allow the bastards to see how hurt and angry she was. Nothing had been gained by doing so, on the contrary, she had lost control, and the last thing she had wanted was to let them get to her.

But get to her they had, not Frederic, the new Dean, who had actually been kind, but Stewart, the new Registrar, Otto's boy, and fat Otto himself, Campus Director, one of Eugene's vile henchmen, Stewart nastily but quietly – she had managed to answer Stewart just as quietly – but when Otto had laced into her, denouncing her, reviling her, accusing her of being contumacious and impertinent, she had lost it and had interrupted him in mid-sentence. This exercise was a charade, she had said, it contravened the union contract, it flew in the face of common decency, he had but to read her evaluations to see whether she was insubordinate or impertinent. But then her voice had cracked and it was all she could do not to burst out crying, the bastard, the fat, ugly bastard.

All three of them, bastards. Maybe Frederic had been kind during the interview but he had gotten into the act before the interview, threatening not to interview her if the union did not withdraw its grievances. When she had refused he had tried a softer approach, if the union withdrew its grievances, he would guarantee that the interview process would be open and aboveboard. Oh, did that mean that the interview process was not going to be open and aboveboard, she had replied. Oh, no, that was not what he had meant, it was just that grievances were confrontational and it would be a good thing to clear the air before the interview. Ah, grievances were confrontational but trampling upon her rights was not, she had replied. Frederic had had no answer to that.

Frederic had been hired while she had been on leave, Hannah having been pushed out by Eugene after he had managed to get rid of most of the other administrators whom he had inherited.

Evidently, Hannah's loyalty during the John Jamieson affair had not saved her.

As for Stewart, he had replaced Reuben as Registrar when Reuben had been promoted to Human Resources, in flagrant disregard of the performance of Derek's assistant of many years, Alison, a close friend of Naomi's, who had applied for the job and whose credentials were outstanding.

Stewart's face had showed no affect but his tone had been aggressive. How would she adapt to new procedures in the Admissions Office, to a new supervisor, he had asked. Her past record showed how, she had replied, without any trouble. But her voice had gone dangerously thin and dry.

As for Otto, it was true that he had a reputation as a bully, that he went around yelling and blustering at people. But how much better she would have felt about herself if, instead of losing it with him, she had interrupted him during his rant and had told him coolly to lower his voice otherwise she would refuse to answer him.

But everything you said was true, Lynne had said, the interview was a charade, it did fly in the face of common decency, anyone else would have lost it sooner.

She hated it when she lost her temper, Naomi had replied, it had made her answer in a way she shouldn't have answered and it had stopped her from thinking of the answer she should have given.

No one was expecting her to be Perry Mason, Lynne had replied. And speaking of Perry Mason, did she know a lawyer, it was time to file a complaint with the Human Rights Commission.

CHAPTER 13

Sheila, her lawyer friend, had been right, Naomi thought, everything depended on the quality of the investigator assigned to her case, and the investigator had turned out to be a dud. Gaston Allard had come to a halt at the second sentence of the memo and had not been able to get beyond it. "The memo is clear," he had said.

Be careful, she had cautioned herself, the man has gone off in the wrong direction and disagreeing with him may rile him. "You have to look at the entire memo," she had said as evenly as possible, "look at that third sentence, Mr. Allard, it qualifies the second –"

"I know, I see it, but you haven't been fired, you are still drawing a salary –"

"Yes, but I don't have a position –"

"Of course, you have a position –"

"Not according to the union contract, Mr. Allard. There's a union contract, you see, the memo cannot be read in isolation. Here, let me show you the relevant clauses."

But reading the contract had had no impact on Allard. The man who was supposed to be her advocate was not interested, he was not following her, he had made up his mind. Furthermore, the more she tried to explain, the more she could see she was losing him, she could see it in his eyes, she was being difficult, she was complicating a simple issue, she was bringing in factors that were completely extraneous to the issue.

Worse, she was challenging him, and that was why she had gotten into trouble in the first place, right?

How had this man ever become an investigator for the Human Rights Commission, had he never heard of unions, did he not understand the idea of contracts?

As for the other examples she had given in her deposition about discrimination against women at Penfield - the replacement of Hannah Weir, Academic Dean, by a male, the replacement of one of the Assistant Deans who had been a female by a male, the appointment of a male as Assistant to the Vice-President even though an experienced female with excellent credentials had applied for the position, the appointment of a male as Assistant to the Academic Dean even though an experienced female with excellent credentials had applied for the position, the appointment of a male to the position of Registrar even though an experienced female with superb credentials – her friend Alison - had applied for the position, the downgrading of the position of Director of Recruitment when the incumbent male was replaced by a female - she and Gaston Allard never got around to discussing any of them.

CHAPTER 14

"It doesn't matter," Lynne said when Naomi reported back to her, "Allard won't file his report for a good while. In the meantime it keeps the pressure on Eugene. And now the time has come to play our last card. The time has come to go to the Board of Directors."

The Board of Directors of Penfield College consisted of eighteen members: six representatives of the outside community, four parent representatives, three teacher representatives, two student representatives and three officers of the College - the President, the Academic Dean and the Director of Student Services. New regulations that were coming into effect in November would add one representative from the Professional ranks and one representative from the Support Personnel ranks.

"When the time comes, you'll be the one to run as our representative," Lynne said, "but November is a long way off. There's a Board meeting scheduled for October and I would like us to try to get the question of your position put on the agenda of the October meeting."

CHAPTER 15

She was writing to the Chairman of the Board of Directors, Naomi reminded herself, a man whom she hardly knew and who was not necessarily familiar with union contracts. She had to take this step by step, she had to be brief – no one liked to read long letters – and she had to make her case in point form as much as possible. Words and logic did not matter to Eugene. She could only hope that words and logic would matter to the Chairman and, through him, to the other Board members.

. . . .

Naomi could not get over her own surprise. She had felt it all along, but only writing up her story for a lay person had made it clear. Not only had Eugene trampled upon her union rights, he had breached two different contracts that existed between her and Penfield so that if she had not been legally bound to fight him in labor court, she would have been able to sue the pants off him in civil court.

On the day before she left on her leave, the Human Resources Department had had her sign a new contract which stated that Penfield College retained her services as Coordinator of Admissions. This contract named her annual salary and stated that she was to be on a leave of absence without pay for a period of one full year. After her merit pay increase was approved, a new contract was mailed to her in France. It named her new annual salary but, as in the preceding contract, it stated that Penfield College retained her services as Coordinator of Admissions and that she was on a leave of absence without pay for one full year.

Furthermore, as stipulated in the union contract, in May she wrote the Human Resources Department to inform them that she would be returning from her leave on the agreed-upon date in August. Two weeks later she received a letter from Human Resources confirming receipt of her letter and informing her that all was in order.

So, in a sense, there were three contracts.

She pointed all this out in her letter and then enumerated all that was incomprehensible about Penfield's actions:

that she had received excellent evaluations from two different supervisors, including the present Director of Human Resources when he was Registrar; that she had been granted a merit salary increase while she was on leave, an increase that had been approved by the President himself; that she had excellent working relationships with faculty and staff, to which end she had attached corroborating letters from five faculty members and two staff members; that it was taxpayer's money that paid for a second individual to do her job while she was kept in a non-existent job; that all the steps taken against her contravened her union contract.

Next had come a list of the steps she had taken in an attempt to get redress and the fact that neither a ruling on the grievances she had filed nor the complaint she had deposited with the Human Rights Commission was expected before the spring at the earliest, for which reason she was requesting a special meeting of Penfield's Board of Directors so that they could intervene.

Then had come her conclusion, her cry from the heart, a summary of the contrast between her proven integrity and competence and the unjust and unjustifiable manner in which she had been treated.

Yes, the letter was good. And this time she had allowed a little passion to enter into her writing. But she had kept it down, passion was allowed, outrage was not, even though the enumeration of the facts had rekindled her outrage.

Outrage, anger. Why was it that angry words diminished one's writing, that it was not meet to modify the word 'actions' with the word reprehensible, nor the word 'contravened' with the word blatantly? Because the facts spoke for themselves and judgmental modifiers weakened one's argument? Because readers did not like to be told what to think and strong words on paper became even stronger in the mind, coming across as overkill?

Yes to all of that. But once again it had not been easy to control her bile and not give it full expression.

CHAPTER 16

Why had they bothered, Naomi thought, as she and Andrew Roper left Eugene's office. In r esponse to their letter, the Chairman of the Board of Directors, Seymour Yellin, had suggested that a meeting be set up between her and Eugene to try to settle their dispute. Through Michael Miller, Penfield's Secretary-General, Seymour's confidante and a close friend of Lynne and Charles, she knew that Eugene had not wanted this meeting, that Eugene had resisted the idea angrily but that it had been forced on him.

There they had been, the two sides, Eugene and Reuben on behalf of Penfield, she and Andrew on her behalf, and they had not gotten anywhere.

But it had been interesting.

Interesting, no, it had been an eye-opener, an education, surreal. If she had not been so directly involved, she would have laughed out loud, that's how absurd Eugene had been.

This had been her first opportunity to observe Eugene from up close and what she had seen was pure glibness at work, a magician who drew arguments out of a hat and words out of the air, someone who danced and skated in all directions but who refused to give up his routine even though this placed him in an impossible position.

According to Eugene, Penfield had assumed at the moment of granting Naomi her leave that Naomi would not be returning to her position, after all, no one had made any verbal assurances to Naomi to that effect, had they, because if they had, he would have felt bound to honor such a commitment. Furthermore, conditions had changed while she was away, there was a new Academic Dean and a new Registrar, and this had lead the College to make changes in the Admissions Office as well. Finally, the selection committee struck to hire a new Coordinator of Admissions had not recommended Naomi for the job and he, Eugene, never tampered with recommendations of selection committees.

Eugene had then suggested that the union put aside their grievances and human rights complaints and concentrate on finding a productive way to use Naomi in the College. The College thought highly of Naomi and was interested in the happiness of its employees – he had actually said that - therefore he would like to find a compromise that would be satisfactory to all sides.

Finally, Eugene had pointed out that should the union stick to technicalities and lose, Naomi would not be in a very good position. On the other hand, if they stuck to technicalities and won, the College could still make changes that could put Naomi back in the position she was in now. That was why it was important to find a compromise. He suggested that Naomi and Andrew meet with Reuben to work out some kind of agreement satisfactory to both sides.

Naomi and Andrew met with Reuben the next day. At the meeting Reuben offered Naomi the position of Coordinator of Athletics. Andrew jumped right in to protest. Reuben couldn't just offer Naomi that position, the position had to be posted and proper hiring procedures had to be followed.

Besides, Naomi had said, she did not feel qualified for this position.

Of course, she was qualified, Reuben had said, he had seen how she had run the Admissions Office. Naomi was more than capable of taking on new responsibilities.

Oh, she had replied, if Reuben was so confident that she could handle something she was unfamiliar with and not particularly interested in, why had she not been allowed to return to the job she did know and where she had proven her capabilities?

There had been no answer to this.

Pressed again by Andrew about the irregularity of the offer of the position of Coordinator of Athletics, Reuben had merely repeated it.

Pressed yet again by Andrew on the same issue, Reuben had admitted that Penfield had not previously assigned Naomi to this position because to do so would have contravened the union contract.

Well, finally something that did make sense, Andrew had said.

And the meeting had come to an end.

CHAPTER 17

This was her easiest letter to date, Naomi thought. Passion wasn't necessary, just a plain recounting of the facts, facts, that if she had not been there, she would not have believed.

She started by thanking Seymour for his interest in her case and for arranging a meeting between her and Eugene.

She then proceeded to demolish all of Eugene's arguments.

To the argument that no one had ever made any verbal assurances to her that the position of Coordinator of Admissions was hers, she pointed out that she had never maintained that anyone had. She then asked why Eugene would feel obligated to honor a verbal assurance that by its nature was hard to prove but would not feel obligated to honor numerous written proofs of just such an assurance.

To the argument that the decision to post her job was taken because conditions at Penfield had changed, she pointed out that Eugene had had but to look at her evaluations, including the ones made by the man Eugene had seen fit to promote to the position of Director of Human Resources, to lay to rest any doubts about her ability to adjust to a new supervisor. Eugene could also have looked at the reasons he had accorded her a merit salary increase to further allay any doubts about this matter.

To the argument that Eugene did not tamper with the recommendations of selection committees, she offered to cite three instances where he had done precisely that.

To the suggestion that she put aside union 'technicalities', she had pointed out that referring to a union contract as 'technicalities' displayed the same disrespect for contractual obligations in verbal form that Eugene had displayed in his actions.

Regarding Eugene's statement that Penfield College was interested in the happiness of its employees she had had to contain herself, commenting simply that if this were indeed the case, the College, under Eugene's leadership, had found a very strange way of demonstrating that interest.

Finally, regarding the statement that should she stick to union 'technicalities' and win the College could still put her back in the same position she was in now, she had said that she expected the College to accept the decision of the arbitrator and implement it in good faith.

She had then reported on the meeting she and Andrew had had with Reuben and had cited Reuben's admission that the College had not previously assigned her to a professional position because that would have contravened her union contract.

This confirmed her contention, she had pointed out. Given that there had been no changes to her original position, the only professional position the College could guarantee her upon her return was the one she held at the time of her leave.

And she had reiterated her request for a special meeting of the Board of Directors to hear her case, dismissing Eugene's so-called explanations as a risible attempt to defend the indefensible.

Was risible too strong a word, Naomi wondered. She would ask Lynne and Andrew and let them decide.

But Eugene's arguments were risible. Damn it, no, risible was not too strong a word.

CHAPTER 18

When Reuben called to tell Naomi that she was to be reinstated in her job, Naomi received the news blankly. She had heard from Lynne who had heard from Michael that the College's lawyers had told Eugene that he did not have a legal leg to stand on, so she had not been surprised.

She had been neither surprised nor elated. But she had won, why did it not feel like a victory?

Because, as far as she was concerned, this whole business should not have happened.

"Should," Reuben had sniggered when she had said this to him at the end of their conversation, "Naomi, when are you going to learn, there's no such thing as should."

She knew that there was no such thing as should, finding out she was gay after she was married and had had children had taught her that, yet she had not been able to help it, the word had come out of her mouth.

....

Neither Lynne nor Danielle had been able to calm her down after this exchange with Reuben.

....

Sheila had calmed her. She had called Sheila in order to have Sheila review the agreement Reuben had drawn up - Naomi was to be reinstated in her job and her record of employment was to be adjusted to show no interruption of service as Coordinator of Admission, the union was to withdraw its grievances and its complaint to the Human Rights Commission. All this had been straightforward enough but she had wanted the wording checked because she didn't trust herself any more. After discussing the agreement, she had told Sheila about her exchange with Reuben, and Sheila had finally succeeded in soothing her soul, in putting her finger on what had been bothering her.

"Naomi, Eugene did not give you your job back because of the justice of your case, he gave you your job back because it suited him to do so at this time and for no other reason," Sheila had said.

Her background was in history and political science, Naomi thought, she knew about Realpolitik, or, at least, she thought she had known, but she realized that she had not understood the concept until now. Eugene had given her job back for one reason and one reason only, his mandate as President was coming to an end in a year and allowing her case to fester might have threatened his chances of getting his term of office renewed. Furthermore, as the newly elected representative of her Association to Penfield's Board of Directors she would be attending her first Board meeting in two week's time, hence the need to relent now, before she took her seat, rather than later. Right had not mattered at all, only power and exigency had mattered. How could such a pessimistic view of things soothe her, it was so contrary to her way of being?

But it did because it was spot on, because it was undeniable, because that's the way the world – or certainly a part of the world – was, and acknowledging it actually helped.

Part Two

CHAPTER 1

Now, Naomi thought, as she raised her hand to ask the question she had been prepped to ask by a colleague who worked in the Accounting Office. She hoped her voice would not betray the pounding of her heart. So much was at stake here – she needed to make a good impression as the representative of the Professionals, she wanted to open the debate on the issue of the surplus -

"Yes, Naomi," Seymour recognized her.

"I am new to this exercise, Mister Chairman, but there is something I don't understand." Damn it, her voice was high and tight. She forced herself to swallow and forged ahead. "According to what you are saying," Naomi turned to address Paul Hunt, the College Comptroller, who had just presented the previous year's financial statements, "last year we were budgeted to break even but we managed to generate a surplus. From what I have gathered, the year before we were also budgeted to break even and the year before as well, yet in both those years the College also generated a surplus. Can you explain that please?"

"That's a good question, Naomi, and I'll be glad to explain it," Paul replied in that smooth voice of his. "At Penfield we operate on the principle that unless we have the money, we don't spend it."

Rubbish, Naomi thought. But she had given Paul an opening and he was going to run with it.

"The Ministry of Education does fund us a certain amount per student," Paul continued, "but, as I said earlier, the exact number of students is not known until the delete deadline of September 20. We can't wait until we know our exact enrolment before we allocate funds. We operate on the principle of budgetary prudence, we prefer to err on the side of caution rather than on the side of incaution."

Now didn't that sound good, Naomi thought, good and right and honorable. "But if we are cautious every year," she pursued, ah, thank goodness, her voice had returned to normal, "and there is a surplus every year, doesn't this mean that we are being too cautious?" That was the heart of the issue according to her colleague in Accounting. The surpluses were Eugene's secret cache, the place from which had come the money to pay a second salary to her putative replacement, Steven Belair, and from which came the money for Eugene to do as he pleased, to spend without constraints and without having to answer to anyone.

"I don't think there is such a thing as being too cautious when you are dealing with public funds, Naomi," Paul smiled. "We have a responsibility to the taxpayers to be cautious, not to spend what we need not spend, not to spend what we may not have."

Bullshit, Naomi thought. But if she raised her story here, she knew it would not go over very well. That was the trouble with these kinds of discussions, with this kind of venue, you had to stay on the surface of things, you couldn't really say what you thought.

The same thing had happened earlier during the meeting, when Eugene had given his regular report to the Board. Eugene had announced that, unlike many other colleges in the Province, Penfield's unions had not gone out on strike even though this was a negotiation year.

Réal Demers had raised his hand to ask a question. Réal, one of the six external members on the Board, was one of Eugene's people. He had made that clear during the light supper that had preceded the Board meeting when he had come over to Naomi to say hello. "You're the one who went to France for a year, right?" he had asked. "Went with your boyfriend, did you?" he had leered. Naomi's stomach had turned. What would Réal have said if he had known that she had gone with Danielle? What would Eugene have done with that information? Thank goodness homosexuals in Quebec were protected against discrimination. But a lot of good that would have done with the Gaston Allards of this world to defend her. "Does the President have a theory as to why Penfield's unions did not go out on strike?" Réal had asked, feeding Eugene his lines.

"I think you have to assume that our personnel are happy with conditions at Penfield," Eugene had replied. He had then reminded the Board that Penfield College, like all other colleges in the Province, could expect a stagnating enrolment and continued budget cuts but that his administration was pledged to manage the negative effects of this on staff through attrition rather than by layoffs so as to maintain staff morale. Staff morale was of the utmost importance to him, he had said in concluding his report.

Staff morale was of the utmost importance to him, Naomi had thought bitterly. She could have raised her story then, too, but then, too, it would have been in bad form. What made it bad form, because it was personal, because it had happened to her? If someone else were to raise her story, would it still be in bad form?

But as far as the issue of the surplus was concerned, she was stymied. Other than the Stephen Belair example, she didn't know what else to say to keep the discussion going.

Réal raised his hand. "I think this administration is to be congratulated for the way it runs its affairs. I have been an administrator at a school commission. I have served on the boards of two other public institutions and I can tell you that this is the way to run things."

Paul nodded appreciatively towards Réal.

Gwen, one of the three teacher representatives on the Board, raised her hand. "No one here is arguing against budgetary prudence, Réal. What we are questioning is the degree of prudence being exercised by this administration. If you are too prudent, things for which the government gives us money do not get done –"

"For example," Réal interrupted.

Gwen looked at Seymour. "I think Réal is out of order, Mr. Chairman."

"You are out of order, Réal," Seymour said.

Naomi groaned inwardly. Seymour did not know his Robert's rules, he did not know the first thing about how to chair a meeting. The meeting had opened with a clash between Eugene and one of the student representatives over the agenda and it was a good thing Michael Miller, in his role as Secretary-General, was there to provide a steady hand, otherwise the discussion might have turned really nasty.

Eugene had decided he did not want students using the front door entrance of the College, no doubt because his office was nearby and he didn't like the noise and dirt that student traffic brought to the area. Brendon, the representative of the Day Division's student body, had tried to add this item to the agenda but it had been voted down. Not before a long and somewhat acrimonious debate on the matter, however, and not before Seymour had shown his appalling ignorance of the rules. For after Brendon had made the motion, which Gwen had seconded, he had begun to speak to the issue, and Seymour had not known enough to stop him. It was Eugene who had done that. "No, this discussion is out of order," Eugene had objected vehemently, "the item is not yet on the agenda, we have to decide first whether to add it before we can discuss it." Seymour had still not known what to do and had looked to Michael, who was sitting to his right, for verification. Michael had upheld Eugene and the discussion about whether to add the item to the agenda had then followed.

The discussion had been about procedures rather than about the issue, but it had been enough to show Naomi who stood where on the Board – the Board to which she had hoped to bring her case. For surely Alain Nadeau, another external representative on the Board, would have used the same argument against hearing her case as he had used against adding the student access item to the agenda. "We can't have every little internal dispute cluttering up the agenda of the Board," Alain had argued, "we meet eight times a year – no, I don't think this item should be added to the agenda." Philip Sauro, another external member, had agreed. "This is a petty matter. I don't think it belongs on the agenda of the Board."

How did people come up with the arguments they used, Naomi had wondered? Did they really think this way or did they just use whatever arguments came to them at the moment? Eugene had barred students from using the main entrance of the College, students, the raison d'être of Penfield, and the item could not make it onto the agenda because Eugene didn't want it there and there were enough people on the Board who went along with him. Not a majority, thank goodness, because a majority had voted to add the item to the agenda, but a two thirds majority was needed to modify the agenda and their side had not gotten that number of votes.

And Seymour had not known this rule nor did he seem to know any of the myriad other rules you needed to know in order to chair a meeting properly, including when to rule people out of order.

"As I was saying," Gwen continued, "if you are too prudent, things for which there is money don't get done even though a surplus is being generated. This leads to another important question, how is surplus money spent? I've been on the Board for three years now and I don't remember ever seeing a reference to surplus money in any budget that was presented to us.

Where is that money? Who decides how that surplus money is spent? Why is the surplus not reflected in the budget that is presented to us?"

Atta girl, Gwen, Naomi thought. She would never have known to ask these kinds of questions.

Alain raised his hand. "We are discussing financial statements this evening, Gwen, not the budget."

"I remember asking a question about surpluses during the budget discussion," Gwen said, anger in her voice, "and I was told then that since the College was not projecting a surplus, my question was premature. Now that the financial statements are showing a surplus and I ask the same question, I am told that the question belongs under the budget discussion."

Beautiful, Naomi thought. She wished she could cheer out loud.

"I hear you, Gwen," Paul said. "But what you have before you is exactly what the government requires, a statement of income and expenses. The statement as presented here is also exactly what the auditor requires."

"So what you are saying is that the surplus does not have to be accounted for," Gwen pursued.

"The surplus sits in the bank and makes money for us," Paul said, "you can see it on page one under line seventeen – it is accounted for –"

"But is the amount of the surplus the same amount as the year before –"

"Of course not, it has gone up by the amount of this year's surplus," Paul said.

Réal guffawed.

Gwen glared at Réal. "I will reword my question, Paul," Gwen said, "even though I think you understood me perfectly the first time, and I would appreciate a proper answer this time. Does our accumulated surplus to date equal last year's accumulated surplus plus this year's?"

"I don't understand your problem, Gwen," Paul said. "Would you prefer that we be in a deficit situation, that the College be placed under trusteeship, is that what you would like?"

Nice dodge, Paul, Naomi thought, but you haven't answered Gwen's question. Did anyone else notice, she wondered. And did the other quieter, external members of the Board understand what was at stake here? Réal and Alain obviously did.

Alain raised his hand. "I would like to remind my fellow Board members that the College was in a deficit situation before Eugene became president. Eugene has wiped out the deficit and has put us in a surplus position. Why are we not applauding this accomplishment? Why are we carping about it?"

That was good, Naomi thought, much as it pained her to admit it.

"I am not carping," Gwen said, "I am asking for transparency. And to that end, I would like to make a motion, that the Comptroller prepare a detailed breakdown of surplus expenditures to date as well as a statement of the policies according to which money from the surplus is disbursed."

Thank goodness for Gwen, Naomi thought. She had known enough to ask the question, but she would not have known to push it the way Gwen had, or to wrap up the discussion by making the kind of motion Gwen had just made. It took a kind of thinking different from hers, less personal, more dispassionate, the kind of thinking she was going to have to learn if she were going to be effective on the Board.

Timothy Evans-Hall seconded the motion. Timothy, another external member, was the previous Chairman of the Board and, according to Lynne, had become completely disenamored with Eugene. Timothy had also voted to add the student access item to the agenda.

So Timothy was a solid ally, Naomi thought. Would that he were a little more aggressive about it, that he were a little more like Réal or Alain.

There was no further discussion. The motion passed, and a few minutes later, the meeting was adjourned.

The Board, Naomi thought as she drove home, there was no such thing as the Board, there were only twenty individual people.

Twenty individual people, the fault line between whom had become very clear during the meeting. First there was us, with Seymour at the head, inept as he was – even in giving his report, he was inept, droning on and on about the different committees he sat on. In addition to Seymour, there were Timothy, Michael, who, under his other hat, that of Director of Student Services, was a voting member of the Board, the three teachers, Carl, Gwen and Vivian, Shant, representative of the Support Personnel, Brendon, the student, and herself. That made nine.

There was them, Eugene, Frederic, Réal, Alain, Philip Sauro and Louise, the other student representative. Eugene had outsmarted them on that one. She and Lynne had realized too late that the election for the Evening Division student was coming up and they had not thought to get anyone they knew to stand. Louise worked for the Regional College Council, a consultative body that grouped together the senior management of all the colleges in the Montreal area – there went one crucial vote for Eugene when the vote for his renewal came up. Then there were the undecided, Irene, the sixth external representative, and the four parent representatives – Dorothy, Jeremiah, Kevin and Walter. Dorothy, Jeremiah and Kevin had voted to add the student access item to the agenda, Irene and Walter, as well as Louise, who obviously had some sense, had abstained. So on the student access item, they had had a majority. But that did not mean that they would hold onto this majority when the time came to vote on the renewal of Eugene's mandate.

That's what all this counting was about, of course. Eugene's mandate as president of Penfield College was coming to an end in December, a year away. The twenty sitting Board members less Eugene would be the ones making the decision about the renewal, since every member's term had either just begun or had enough time to run beyond December. It looked like their side had a good start on the numbers, but they needed ten votes, not nine, and student access was not as important an issue as Eugene's mandate. There was no guarantee that Dorothy, Jeremiah and Kevin would be onside when the vote on Eugene's mandate came around.

That was why it had been so important to make a good impression, to get to know the people a little. Well, the meeting had gone well, she and Gwen had made a great tandem, that boded well, Naomi thought.

If only she could get her stomach under control – she had been nervous all day, had gotten the runs just before the meeting - but she had settled down once the meeting had begun, although she had had some trouble with her voice.

But that was normal, when she felt passionately about things, the passion took over. She had to learn to keep the passion under control, to be cool, not hot, to think, not emote. In other words, she had to turn her thinking inside out, to stop thinking about how bad Eugene and his minions were and just listen to their words and turn their words against them. It was not going to be easy, it was not something that came naturally to her.

It came naturally to Alain. Alain was a lawyer, maybe that was why.

Funny about Alain, he sat next to her and they had bantered in a most warm, friendly way before the meeting had started. But once the meeting had started he had turned into a barracuda.

No, that was not the way to think, she had to remember to stick to the issues, not to personalities.

She would have to make that her mantra, the issues, not the personalities.

CHAPTER 2

"I don't trust Gwen," Lynne said the next day over lunch, "I don't trust Gwen and I don't trust Carl."

"Oh, oh, Lynne, if we can't trust those two, then –"

"That's why I said you have to work on the undecided, on Dorothy, on Irene, on Louise, on Gwen."

"Louise is a lost cause, Lynne, I'm sure of it."

"You have to try."

"As for Gwen, she was terrific last night –"

"So Michael said. He said that the two of you made a great team."

"But you don't trust her."

"No, I do not. I don't trust her and I don't trust the teacher's union. The teachers running the union have always had a very narrow corporatist outlook, all that matters are the little games that they play, and Gwen is a union person, as is Carl. That's why I think it's going to be close, very close. In the meantime, we have to start working on our submission to the Board."

"Oh, god, more writing."

"I'm afraid so."

"I know this is going to sound like a stupid question, Lynne, but when you say work on Dorothy and Irene, what exactly do you mean?"

"I mean get to know them, go to lunch with them, schmooze with them."

"I don't think I'm very good at that kind of thing."

"Just be yourself, Naomi, you'll be fine."

CHAPTER 3

She had been herself, Naomi thought, as she drove back to the office after having had lunch with Dorothy, but, as far as she was concerned, that had not been good enough. Because the same qualms that had paralyzed her at the Board had paralyzed her with Dorothy. Eugene is a bastard, she had felt like saying, but had not. How could she?

Did she fear that, as the wronged party, she would come over as the one with an axe to grind, whose judgment was off? Wouldn't that have been the case if, after he had given his report, she had asked Eugene whether his treatment of her was an example of how he maintained staff morale at Penfield? Inappropriate, Alain would have said, let's keep the personal out of this.

Would she have had the presence to answer, sorry, Alain, this is not personal, this is about a flagrant example of how not to maintain staff morale? Or if she had asked Paul whether hiring Steven Belair as her replacement was an example of the College's not spending what it need not spend? Or better, whether Steven Belair's totally unnecessary salary had come from the surplus that never got accounted for? Confrontational, Alain would have said, personal vendettas have no place at the Board.

That was it, she was afraid that what she had to say would be seen as personal – as a victim, everything she had to say was personal, wasn't it - the personal could be dismissed as such, and she had neither the quick repartee nor the steely stomach to make it be seen otherwise.

Then there was the fact that, although not written into the agreement, she had understood Reuben to say when they had negotiated her reinstatement that the College considered her case to be closed. Meaning what, that she was not allowed to talk about it? Would Eugene have attacked her for breaching this unwritten understanding? What would she have answered to that? That this was a free country? No, she did not have the stomach for that either. What had happened was still too raw, had thrown her too completely for her to have gained control over her feelings and she knew herself, she would have ended up crying.

Which is why she had said nothing at the Board.

As for Dorothy, she was a lovely woman, warm, kind, but totally without political experience and she had been afraid to push too hard.

She had started by finding out a little about her. Dorothy's youngest son was the one who was a student at Penfield, her older son was at university. Naomi would have loved to talk to Dorothy about her girls, it would have helped create a bond between them but she didn't think she could risk telling Dorothy that her daughters lived with their father. She had then found out how Dorothy had come to sit on the Board - Dorothy had decided that the time had come to get a little more involved in the community, so when elections for a Parent representative had come up she had decided to stand. This was her opening and she had asked Dorothy what she thought of her experience on the Board thus far.

"I find it interesting," Dorothy had replied. "I'm not sure I understand all the issues all of the time, but then again I've just been on the Board since September."

"Well, as an internal member of the Board who knows quite a bit about what is going on at the College, you can ask me about any issue you like," she had replied. "I know you might be wary of me because I am an internal member, but all I can say is that I will do my best to answer all of your questions honestly and fairly."

"That's very kind of you," Dorothy had said, "I believe you and feel very comfortable with you, but surely you will understand if I say that

I feel I have to figure things out on my own. I'm sure you would be the same way."

"Yes," she had replied, refusing to give up quite yet, "except that I have learned that sometimes others can speed up our learning, help us figure things out more quickly – the thing to do is to find people you are comfortable with, whose judgment you can trust." And she had let it go at that. She felt she had gone as far as she could with Dorothy, to have said more might have alienated her.

CHAPTER 4

Ugly, Naomi cried on the way home, ugly, ugly, ugly. There was no other word to describe them, Eugene, Alain and Réal were ugly, ugly, ugly people.

And she was not thinking physically, although Eugene had pasty features and a round, shapeless body and Réal looked like a toad, with his round bald head, beady eyes and thin wide mouth.

Only Alain was physically presentable, but their pugnaciousness, their shamelessness made them morally and spiritually repugnant to her.

This was the meeting that had had as its main agenda item The Renewal of the President's Term of Office, discussions about which were going to be held in camera. All the preliminary items, Business Arising, The Chairman's Report – even Seymour had droned on less than usual – and The President's Report had been disposed of and they had come to the main item of business.

Seymour had looked up and in his low voice had solemnly asked the visitors to leave the room. The thirteen or fourteen people who had been sitting in the visitors' seats had gotten up and had filed out of the room. Then the doors had closed and silence had fallen. Eugene had not moved from his seat.

And that's when the ugliness had begun.

Timothy had lead the charge, totally ineptly, unfortunately. "I thought these discussions were being held in camera," Timothy had said, "shouldn't the President have left the room?"

"I'm staying," Eugene had snapped, making no attempt to mollify Timothy, to meet him even part way.

"That's ridiculous," Timothy had said. He had turned to Seymour. "How can we have an open discussion about this item when the President is present?"

Alain's hand had shot up. "The law gives the President the right to participate in the discussions. He does not have a vote but he may participate in the discussions."

"May participate does not mean should participate," Timothy had said, standing up. "It's indecent, that's what it is."

"The law gives me the right to participate and I have every intention of availing myself of this right," Eugene had declared.

What a bastard, Naomi had thought. When the law said Eugene *could* participate it became a right, but when a written union contract *guaranteed* her job it was dismissed as a technicality.

"I've never heard of anything so ridiculous in my life," Timothy had said, "and I have no intention of participating in such a travesty." He had stood up and had begun to gather up his papers.

"Please, Timothy," Vivian had entreated, "if the rules allow the President to be present during the discussion, then they allow it. You have to stay."

"Yes, Timothy," Dorothy had said, "please."

And Timothy had sat down.

Had Timothy really thought that his gesture would move Eugene? Not good, Naomi had thought, not good. It needed a cool mind to take on Eugene, heat and anger wouldn't do it. She knew this, how come Timothy did not know it?

Gwen had raised her hand. "Mr. Chairman, are you familiar with this rule?"

"No," Seymour had said, "I am not. But if –"

Shant had raised his hand. "I would like to make a motion, that the Chairman be authorized to ask Penfield's lawyer to verify this rule and report back to us at the next meeting."

"Are you saying that the President does not know the rules?" Alain had asked.

"The motion has not been seconded," Michael had reminded everyone.

"Does anyone second Shant's motion?" Seymour had asked.

"I do, I second the motion," Vivian had raised her hand.

"Is there any discussion?" Seymour had asked.

"It's an insulting motion to make," Réal had said, "this is not the way to start a delicate process of this kind –"

Yeah, right, Naomi had thought. Suddenly the process that Eugene, Alain and he had started in a most indelicate manner had become delicate.

"It's because the process is so delicate that this step must be taken," Shant had said, not waiting to be recognized by Seymour, "we need to be sure –"

"Do you think the President would insist on this if he weren't sure," Alain had said.

"Probably not," Shant had agreed, "but why didn't the President inform the Chairman and the entire Executive Committee, of which Timothy is a member, of this rule before?"

"The Chairman and the Board have been informed at the appropriate time –"

"You call this appropriate," Shant had not let Alain finish, "that you knew but the Chairman and the rest of the Board did not know? What do we have here, two different classes of Board members, one member who is informed before a meeting of a most important rule and all the others, including the Chairman, who are kept in the dark?"

"I call the question," Gwen had said.

Seymour looked at Michael.

"This means that the vote goes ahead without further discussion," Michael had said.

The vote was taken. Alain, Frederic, Louise, Philip and Réal voted against, Irene, Michael and Walter abstained, Eugene and Seymour did not vote, everyone else voted for. The motion passed.

A long silence had followed. Were people digesting what had happened, Naomi had wondered. Were they marveling at the wanton belligerence they had just witnessed? Too bad Timothy was not like Shant, Shant had been wonderful, and he had taken Eugene on in the only way possible, legally, not by making useless gestures.

Timothy had raised his hand. "I would like to make a motion, that a committee be struck by the Board to consider the matter of the reappointment of the President. This committee will be presided over by the Chairman and shall consist of six other Board members, three representing external constituencies and three representing internal constituencies. This committee will seek the advice and input of the Pedagogical Council, Penfield's highest consultative body, and will submit its report as well as the recommendations of the Pedagogical Council to the Board by Friday, March 29."

Dorothy had raised her hand. "I second the motion."

So Timothy had talked to Dorothy. This was positive, Naomi had thought. Maybe if she couldn't get Dorothy onside, Timothy could.

Alain had raised his hand. "I'm against the motion. I'm against the make-up of the committee, it's too restrictive. I'm against the time-line, it's too long."

Unbelievable, Naomi had thought, the man didn't give an inch.

Réal had raised his hand. "I agree with Alain. What counts is to have the best people on the committee, you can't decide in advance that there should be so many external members and so many internal members –"

They were sickening, Naomi had thought, and she had raised her hand. "The make-up of Timothy's committee represents the make-up of this Board. There are ten external members and ten internal members –"

"I don't like it," Alain had said, "I don't see what is to be gained by a committee reporting back to us when I am not bound by what the committee recommends –"

"Are you saying, Alain," Shant has asked, "that if, for the sake of argument and unlikely as it is, the committee were to submit a unanimous recommendation, be it affirmative or negative, you would not go along with that recommendation?"

"I'm saying that I do not delegate my right to make up my mind to anyone, unanimity notwithstanding," Alain had said.

"Me neither," Réal had said.

"Furthermore, I find the time-line much too long," Alain had said. "Today is February 12, there is no way this thing should be allowed to drag on to the end of March –"

"The President's term of office is not up until December 31st of this year," Gwen had said, "there is lots of time –"

"It's too long, it's too contentious, it's not good for the College," Réal had said.

"Mr. Chairman, are we discussing the creation of the committee or the time-line?" Walter had asked.

"We are discussing the creation of the committee," Seymour had said.

"Well, it doesn't look as if we're getting anywhere, does it?" Walter had said, looking at his watch.

The meeting had started at seven o'clock, it was now nine o'clock.

Walter had abstained on several votes to date, Naomi had thought, but she had a sinking feeling that he was leaning towards Eugene. Damn.

Timothy had raised his hand. "I made this motion because I thought it was a fair way to proceed. As Naomi pointed out, the composition of the proposed committee reflects the composition of this Board. As Gwen pointed out, the time-line is fair. In the corporate world where I come from, this is the procedure that would be followed."

"That may be how things work in the corporate world, Timothy," Alain had said, "but this is a much smaller and much more democratic environment than the corporate world and, as such, your idea of a committee is not useful here. The committee will have to report to the Board, but the committee's recommendation will not bind me or anyone else who will not have been on the committee. I will want to know why the committee came to the conclusion it came to and the whole process will start all over again. I'm against your motion, I think it will be a waste of everyone's time, I think we need something more adapted to our environment."

Carl had raised his hand. "I would like to make a motion."

"Yes?" Seymour had said.

"There is a motion on the floor," Michael had said.

"Of course, yes," Seymour had said.

Moron, Naomi had thought. Why didn't Seymour go home and memorize Robert's Rules of Order. He was Chairman, for god's sake.

"I call the question," Vivian had said.

"We are voting on Timothy's motion," Seymour had said. "All those in favour?"

Brendon, Dorothy, Shant, Timothy, Vivian and she had voted for, Alain, Frederic, Irene, Louise, Philip, Réal, and Walter had voted against, Carl, Gwen, Jeremy, Kevin and Michael had abstained, Eugene and Seymour had not voted. The motion was defeated.

Carl had raised his hand. "I would like to make a motion, that from now until the end of March the Board receive briefs and/or oral presentations from all interested sectors of the Penfield community concerning the renewal of the President's term of office that it will hear and consider as a Committee of the Whole. The Board will also seek the advice of the Pedagogical Council on the matter."

Alain's hand had shot up. "Too long, much too long."

"The motion has not been seconded," Michael had said.

Gwen had raised her hand. "I second the motion."

"Too long," Réal had said, "I agree with Alain, it's entirely too long a time period. I would like to propose an amendment, that the time period be changed from the end of March to March 8."

"I second the motion," Alain had said.

"Absolutely not," Shant had said. "Today is February 12 and you want to give the community a total of three weeks to prepare briefs on a matter of such importance? Three weeks is not enough time."

"But then we have to hear these briefs, you'll have us sitting until June," Walter had said.

"Exactly. Every effort should be make to expedite this matter, not to drag it out," Alain had said.

Naomi had raised her hand. "Mister Chairman, I thought I just heard Alain argue against Timothy's motion because it was not sufficiently adapted to the democratic environment that prevails here as compared to the corporate world." She had then turned to Alain. "How can you now argue in favor of curtailing the expression of opinion by the various bodies that constitute this democratic environment?"

"Touché," Gwen had said. "I call the question."

Alain, Philip, Réal and Walter had voted in favour of the amendment, Brendon, Carl, Dorothy, Gwen, Irene, Jeremy, Kevin, Michael, Shant, Timothy, Vivian and she had voted against, Frederic and Louise had abstained, Eugene and Seymour had not voted. The amendment was defeated.

"I call the original question," Vivian had said.

This motion had passed without difficulty, the date and time of the next meeting had been set and the meeting had been adjourned.

Was there any other way to describe Eugene and Alain and Réal but as ugly, Naomi thought. Months before they had needed to they had started the 'delicate' process in a most indelicate manner, which they had then tried to curtail time-wise and discussion-wise, with Alain and Réal defending their position in the same let's-pull-an-argument-out-of-the-hat manner that Eugene had used with her. The only difference between the three of them was in their manner, Eugene displaying his true nature - truculent and nasty - when Timothy had asked why Eugene had not left the Boardroom, Alain handling himself very smoothly, while Réal fell somewhere in the middle, he was a real little me-too, Réal was, following Eugene's and Alain's lead obediently. But whether rough or smooth, the three of them gave no quarter, they were grasping, combative, ugly, ugly people.

CHAPTER 5

At least she wouldn't be writing the brief all by herself, Naomi thought, although she had agreed to edit the final version.

There were three principles she and her colleagues would have to keep in mind, keep it brief, keep it in point form and use the language of management books.

Management books. She had devoured them while sitting in the Academic Dean's area exercising the 'certain duties' she had been assigned.

'Certain duties'. She had actually been given a make-work task while in exile, to write a viewbook for the College. No one else would have done it, given the circumstances, but she had actually written a rather fine work. It just went to show, you could take the girl out of her professional position, but you couldn't take the professionalism out of the girl.

But the view book had not been enough to keep her busy. And even if it had been, she would have found the time to read her management books. Because what had happened to her had turned her world upside down – not quite as much as finding out she was gay, but close – and she had needed to try to make sense of it. And she had found herself following the same pattern she had followed then, reading voraciously on the subject, keeping a diary and thinking - obsessing – about her situation. That was it, she obsessed when she didn't understand and kept a diary when she lost control and tried desperately to regain it.

She did not go anywhere without her diary lest she forget to do something, call someone, lest she forget an idea she had had. She wasn't as tortured as she had been when she had discovered she was gay, but her whole waking existence was consumed by her situation – first in trying to get her job back, and now in trying to remove Eugene from office.

She had even put her fiction writing aside – to her great disappointment, she hadn't made any progress on her half-finished novel during the year she had spent in France, but Reuben's phone call at the end of July had stopped her from working any further on that undertaking for now.

As for reading, she had read and read and read but Eugene's management style was not to be found anywhere. The books described an ideal world in which presidents worked for the good of their companies, in which different management styles – the consensual versus the authoritarian – were weighed and analyzed. She had searched and searched but had not found anyone resembling Eugene in any of the case studies she had come across. Were businesses never run by tyrants? Was it only at Penfield that the likes of a Eugene were to be found?

Then she had come across a business book written by a British political scientist and things had begun to make more sense. The answers to a Eugene were not to be found in business books, which were written by people delighted with their own jargon and caught up in the belief that they were describing something other than human nature – as if business were different from any other human endeavor - but in books written about power and ego and manipulation. And despite having found what she was looking for, the word 'should' had still come out of her mouth when she had gotten her job back, and she had needed Sheila to remind her that what she had been dealing with had been described in Machiavelli, not Peter Drucker.

But despite this, their brief would use management language, because, as she had found, you couldn't say things directly, you had to dress them up. Or was it that the opposition had to dress things up, Eugene and his two side-kicks could say what they had to say bluntly and aggressively.

Aggression had its advantages, it was plain to see, not the least of which was that it put the opposition on the defensive. Here they were, representatives of the three employee groups of the College - Lynne had grave doubts about the teacher's union but she remained hopeful – experts on Eugene's mismanagement of the College – yes, previous administrations had not been as financially responsible, but Eugene was only seemingly financially responsible – put in the unenviable position of having to explain and qualify when what people wanted was brevity and simplicity. But things were not always simple, nor did words always mean what they seemed to mean, or they did, but the person using them did not always use them in an accepted manner -

There she was, falling into the 'should' trap again. What did 'accepted manner' mean for a Eugene, for an Alain, for a Réal –

Was there really such a thing as an accepted manner? Could it be that the meaning of words was only a convention -

She had better watch it, she would lose all sense of right and wrong if she continued along this path. Eugene was a power-hungry man whom she had seen skate and slither and slide in any which direction when it suited him.

As for Alain – maybe he really believed the things he said –

He really was quite personable –

But it didn't matter whether he believed the things he said or not, he was a formidable opponent. In Alain, Eugene had a powerful and able ally.

And in Réal, a reliable deputy.

And on their side they had Seymour and Timothy.

And a very uphill battle on their hands.

CHAPTER 6

Seymour was going to lose it for them, Naomi thought on her way home from that evening's Board meeting. He didn't know the first thing about running a meeting, and what was worse, he wasn't making any effort to learn. He had not known when to introduce the lawyer who had been brought in to settle the question about Eugene's right to be present during the renewal discussions – not at the very outset of the meeting, but under Business Arising, as Eugene had pointed out acidly. He had not remembered to clear the room when calling upon the lawyer since all matters pertaining to these discussions were supposed to be held in camera. He had not known, after the lawyer had left, that the Board had not yet finished with the item. "We come to the next item on the agenda –" he had begun, and Eugene had interrupted him in mid-sentence. "We are not finished with this item. At the last meeting we passed a motion that the Board would sit as a Committee of the Whole. But that's all we did. We did not discuss the modalities of how and when the Committee would sit. We have to set the dates for the special meetings this item is going to need."

A short discussion had ensued and the matter was dealt with, but not before Walter had again shown his impatience with the whole process by suggesting setting aside part of the next regular Board meeting in April for discussion of the briefs.

Jeremy had corrected him gently. "I think we will need more than one meeting," he had said with a smile.

"Unfortunately, Jeremy, I think you're right," Walter had replied. "How about Tuesdays, then," Walter had suggested, "since the regular Board meetings take place on Tuesdays and people are more likely to be available."

"I was going to propose the same thing," Eugene had said. "Shall we say April 9 and April 16?"

"There is a Board meeting scheduled for the 9th," Seymour had said.

"Perfect," Walter had said. "We can have the regular meeting and then the special meeting, can't we?" Walter had asked, addressing himself to Michael.

"Yes," Seymour had answered.

Naomi had cringed. So Seymour had finally known the answer to a procedural question, but he had had to make sure that everyone else knew it too. Dear god, she thought.

The visitors were called back into the room.

"The next item on the agenda –"

Naomi had raised her hand. Her heart was not pounding, she had noted, this was good. "Mister Chairman, I have a question that falls under Business Arising. In December the Board passed a motion instructing the Comptroller to report back to us about the exact amount of money there was in surplus and about the rules governing expenditure from surplus. I would like to ask when we are going to receive this report."

Seymour had turned towards Paul Hunt, but Eugene had answered in his stead. "I know for a fact that the Comptroller is working on this report, but I would remind the Board that there was no date attached to this motion."

Gwen's hand had shot up. "That's as pitiful an excuse as I have ever heard, Mr. Chairman. The next thing we know there won't be any surplus left and no one will have to answer for it because it will have happened before Paul reported back to us."

"Objection," Alain had said. "Are you accusing this administration of spending money it has no right to spend?"

"No, I am not. But to say that we have not yet had a report because there was no date attached to my motion is, as I said, pitiful. I therefore propose attaching a date to that motion now –"

"When can you have your report ready?" Eugene had asked Paul brusquely.

"At the next Board meeting," Paul had replied. "I had intended to have the report ready for this meeting, but the auditors were in and I don't know whether any of you have any idea how long it takes to prepare the files for the auditors, how long it takes to actually review the files with the auditors –"

"Disgusting," Réal had said, "all this bickering."

"Yes," Alain had agreed, "and over nothing too."

And Seymour had done nothing to stop them, Naomi thought. Réal and Alain were out of order, they were poisoning the atmosphere, they had denigrated her and Gwen while at the same time they had disparaged an issue of importance –

Seymour probably didn't understand the issue, come to think of it -

They were involved in a war and their general was a fool.

A fool who had helped her get her job back, for which she would forever be grateful, but a fool, nevertheless.

The next item on the agenda had been the Report of the Personnel Committee. This had been the brainchild of a former member of the Board whose appointment to a government post in Quebec City had necessitated her resignation. The idea had been to establish a permanent sub-committee of the Board whose main function would be to oversee personnel policies pertaining to management staff. With the departure of that member, the Committee now consisted of Eugene and Seymour.

Eugene had taken the floor. He outlined the management structure in place at Penfield and described the two formal operational committees of the College, the Management Committee, which dealt with general administrative questions, and the Academic Policy Committee, which dealt with academic matters, both of which he chaired.

That Eugene chaired the Academic Policy Committee and not Frederic, the Academic Dean, spoke volumes, but no one had remarked on that. Poor Frederic. On a personal level, he was nice enough, but professionally, he was as weak as they came. Which, no doubt, had been the idea when Eugene had hired him. In her mind she had taken to calling Frederic by another name, Before, after the advertisements in the comics years ago for Charles Atlas body-building courses, when *before* he takes the course a young man is a puny fellow and after the course he becomes beautifully muscled. Not nice, on her part, but she couldn't help it. And it did give her some solace to think in these terms.

"Can the President tell us whether the job descriptions of his various directors and managers have been brought up to date?" Timothy had asked. "I seem to recall that that was one of the goals of the Personnel Committee, to ensure that this was done."

"It's in the process of being done. It's not as easy a task as it seems," Eugene had said, "and it's not as if we can stop everything to get it done. The daily needs of the college must be attended to. But I can say that we are in the process of getting it done."

"Another goal of the Personnel Committee," Timothy had said, "was to ensure that there were regular performance reviews of the directors and managers —"

"Yes," Eugene had said, "that will happen as soon as all the job descriptions are updated."

"Are you saying that at present there are no regular performance reviews of the directors and managers?" Kevin had asked. Kevin worked for an engineering consulting firm.

"Of course, we have performance reviews," Eugene had said, "but until now they have been somewhat informal. Once the job descriptions are updated, we will formalize the process."

The remaining items on the agenda were dealt with and the meeting had been adjourned.

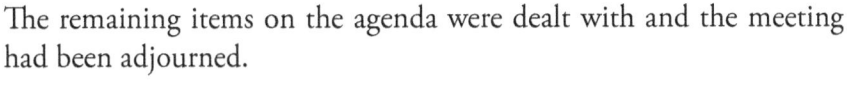

"Informal performance reviews, my eye," Lynne said the next morning when Naomi reported to her about the evening's goings-on. "Charles has not had a performance review since Eugene became president. The man lies."

"Convincingly, I am sorry to say. If I didn't know what I know, I would have believed Eugene, too. I'm sure all the external members believed him."

"Not Timothy."

"No, not Timothy. And, of course, not Seymour. And Kevin did not seem impressed. I think Kevin may have become ours last night. I sure hope so."

CHAPTER 7

"**W**as it for this that this special meeting was called," Alain thundered, "for this?"

"The auditor's report merits our full attention," Seymour insisted. "All the inadequacies mentioned in this report have to be addressed. It is our responsibility as directors of a public institution to ensure that Penfield College is run in the most professional, in the most irreproachable manner."

"And where in the auditor's report is there any implication that the College is not being run this way?" Réal asked.

"Has the chairman never seen an auditor's report before?" Alain asked. "Auditors always find fault with a company's or an institution's procedures, that's their job to find fault. But in this instance nothing the auditors say is of a serious nature."

"I believe and continue to believe that this report merits our closest attention," Seymour said.

"What are your thoughts on this matter, Mr. President? You must have discussed this report with Mr. Hunt," Réal said.

"I did," Eugene said. "And if the Chairman had given me the chance, I would have discussed the report with him as well."

"Did I hear you correctly, Mr. President? Are you saying that the Chairman did not discuss the report with you?" Alain asked.

"That is correct," Eugene replied.

"And so this special meeting of the board was called by the Chairman without consulting you?"

Alain asked.

"Yes, it is the Chairman's prerogative to call special meetings of the Board," Eugene said.

"Just as it is the President's prerogative to set the agendas of the regular meetings," Brendon said.

"What does setting the agenda have to do with this?" Réal asked.

"Some of us don't like that a special meeting has been called," Brendon said. "Well, some of us don't like the way the agenda is set –"

"Since we are here," Timothy said, "I propose that we get on with it, that we deal with the auditor's report."

"I agree with Timothy," Vivian said, "but Brendon has a point. I know that this is not the time, but I would like to discuss the setting of the agendas of Board meetings at a later date –"

"She's out of order, Mr. Chairman," Alain said, "there is only one item on our agenda this evening –"

"Please," Kevin said, "let's all try to relax a little. I agree with the last three speakers, let's get on with it, let's look at the way the Board's agenda is set at a later date, and," Kevin smiled at Alain, "I guess I'm out of order, too."

She was sure of it now, Naomi thought, Kevin had come over to their side. He knew enough about meetings and organizations not to have been intimidated by the Gang of Three - Eugene and Alain and Réal – and to see the issues for what they were.

"Perhaps the Auditor can start by summarizing the most important points of his report," Timothy suggested.

The Auditor proceeded to speak to his report, there were few questions and the meeting was adjourned within an hour.

God, Seymour was inept, Naomi thought on her way home, what had been the point of all that? She knew that Seymour confided in Michael and that Michael was trying his best to guide Seymour, but Seymour was either unwilling or unable to absorb what Michael was telling him. Besides, Michael could not guide Seymour in everything. At some point, Seymour himself had to get it. Well, he wasn't getting it, he wasn't getting it at all.

CHAPTER 8

This was the best she could do, Naomi thought. Had she succeeded in communicating Eugene's style, in communicating the essence of the man – although, in Eugene's case, style was the essence. She hoped – she thought - she had. She had worked and worked and worked and had finally succeeded in cutting down her Association's brief from twenty-five pages – twenty-five pages – to ten.

She leafed through the document slowly. Yes, she had used management concepts to organize its content. Under Objectives, she had slammed Eugene for having opened a branch of Penfield College downtown whose sole purpose was to run programs for business. There had been no consultation and no feasibility study, she had pointed out, plus Penfield would be competing with two universities and three other colleges for the market in that area. How did opening this branch coincide with Penfield's basic mission, of providing post-secondary education to high school graduates and young adults, she had then asked.

Under the same item, she had slammed Eugene for decreeing that the Admissions Office test the English proficiency of all applicants, irrespective of their linguistic background. This would have meant testing six thousand applicants as opposed to the approximate two hundred applicants they usually tested. When asked why he wanted to do this, Eugene's curt reply had been, to develop a statistical base. A statistical base for what purpose? The latter question was never answered and the idea was abandoned only after staff and faculty spent weeks pleading with Eugene not to proceed.

Of course she had mentioned the fact that students had been barred from using the main entrance of the College. She had also mentioned that students had not been invited to the ceremony inaugurating the new Sports Complex. Who was this college for anyway, she had asked.

Under Planning, she had blasted Eugene for moving Student Services from its original, prime location to an ill-suited area in the basement in what had been student space. The move had ended up costing much more than anticipated and depriving students of that space since the area vacated by Student Services was turned into a lounge and meeting room. Once again, there had been no consultation, all had been done by Presidential fiat.

She had also raised the issue of the surplus, pointing out that Penfield was not the only college in Quebec to show a surplus but that it was the only one where the amount of the surplus and the rules for its expenditure were a tightly guarded secret.

Under Decision-making, she had described her case, of course, but she had also described another disastrous personnel decision take by Eugene, that of having hired a new head of Information Systems without having checked the man's references, none of which, it turned out after the fact, had been favorable. Staff complaints had begun immediately but were systematically ignored. The man left suddenly a year after he was hired, but consultants had had to be hired at a cost of over $60,000 to repair the damage that had been inflicted on the Student Records System.

Under Communication and Consultation, she had denounced the fact that in the one instance where there had been ready-made consultation waiting to be utilized it had been ignored. Six different services and departments were relocated this past summer, including Student Services, but none of those changes had been recommended by the Space Committee, which had submitted its report the previous December. Needless to say, the two most pressing space needs identified by the Committee had not been addressed.

Then there had been the Presidential decree, issued late last June, that Penfield offer its remedial English courses in the summer rather than in the fall. There was nothing wrong with this decision other than that it had been taken much too late to be implemented that summer. A reasonable person would have seen this immediately. In Eugene's case, postponement was achieved only after days and days of pleading for a delay until the following year.

Under Motivation and Leadership, she had briefly referred to her case but had elaborated at length about the case of her friend and colleague, Alison. Talented, innovative and very experienced in all areas pertaining to the position, Alison had neither been appointed Interim Registrar when the position had become vacant nor hired permanently when her name was put forward by the Hiring Committee as the best person for the position. Alison, like Naomi, had received a merit pay increase six months before applying for the Registrar's position. Why had the President not appointed this superbly qualified employee to this position, she had asked.

Her Conclusion had been succinct. Penfield needed a president who understood that students were Penfield's raison d'être, that faculty and staff were Penfield's top resource, and whose goal was to serve the cause of education rather than the other way around. The Professional Association was unanimous in its opinion that Eugene Guzman was not that man and urged the Board not to renew his mandate as President of Penfield College.

CHAPTER 9

Lynne had been right, Naomi thought. Weeks earlier Lynne had said she didn't trust Gwen and Carl. Well, she didn't know about Carl, but she now knew about Gwen. What a painful lunch that had been. She and Gwen might make a good team at the Board, but what she had come up against in the woman was a brick wall. "Every academic department is against Eugene's renewal," she had pointed out.

"The departments have their concerns, the Union has its concerns," Gwen had replied. "Penfield has expanded under Eugene's presidency, this has been good for the teachers, it has lead to more jobs."

"Penfield's expansion has had nothing to do with Eugene," she had countered, "and I should know, don't you think? It's my job to know. All the colleges – English and French both - are bursting at the seams. But the demographics are going to change for the worse, and very soon, too – can you see Eugene as the man to manage attrition?"

"Well, Seymour certainly couldn't."

"What does Seymour have to do with it?"

"He's angling for the Presidency," Gwen had said.

"Seymour? Since when is this a contest between Eugene and Seymour?" she had asked. "The two of them can't stand each other and they're both on a power trip, but not renewing Eugene's mandate does not mean Seymour becomes President."

"I think you're being naïve," Gwen had said.

"Seymour does not have a chance in hell of becoming President and you know it, Gwen. Seymour is not the issue, Eugene is the issue. The man has never done anything that did not suit him personally, he has no vision beyond his personal power. He has been going around offering money to the Departments as if there is no tomorrow – suddenly there is money for all the things that teachers and Departments have been complaining about for years – money from the surplus, no doubt, the money you and I have tried to get at –"

"I'm not saying that Eugene is wonderful," Gwen had said, "all I'm saying is that he can be worked with, he understands teachers' issues –"

"That's not what the departments are saying," she had said, ending up right back where she had started. What else could she have said? According to Gwen there were the departments – eleven academic departments had submitted briefs and they had all been unanimous in their condemnation of Eugene - and there was the Teachers' Union. Meaning that teachers and Teachers were not synonymous. Meaning that the Teachers' Union could not care less what its members said via the departments and that the Union had taken a position different from theirs. Meaning that of the three teacher representatives on the Board, the precious votes of the two teachers who represented the Union – Gwen and Carl - were not in the bag. Meaning that even though two years earlier Eugene had so enraged the Union that they had gone out on a five-week wildcat strike, the Union had since worked out a modus vivendi with the man.

She wondered what goodies the Union was hankering for - more release time for Union executive members, more input from the Union on College business, a looser interpretation of contractual rules? One thing was certain, academic concerns were not on the Union's agenda.

She felt sick to her stomach.

CHAPTER 10

Naomi took her seat at the Boardroom table. Tonight was the night hearings about the renewal of Eugene's term of office would begin. If only her stomach would stop churning, if only she weren't so nervous, so tense...

"The two hundred and fortieth regular meeting of the Board of Directors of Penfield College is called to order," Seymour intoned. "The first item is Approval of the Agenda."

Vivian raised her hand. "As a follow-up to our discussion at the Special Meeting two weeks ago, I would like to add the item, Setting the Agenda."

"Here we go again," Alain said.

Kevin raised his hand. "I would be interested in hearing what Vivian has to say."

Eugene nodded his head very slightly.

Seymour hesitated.

"Can we get on with it, Mr. Chairman," Alain said.

So, Naomi thought, Kevin's comment had carried. How much more clout the outsiders had than the insiders. Or the non-committed votes than the committed votes.

And how well Eugene and Alain communicated, Naomi added a moment later.

"Please continue, Vivian," Seymour said.

"I think the item, Varia, should be added as a standing item to the Board's agenda," Vivian said. "This would allow members to bring questions or issues to the Board that they are interested in, it would open up the discussion a little."

"And create a free-for-all," Alain said.

"Democracy, Alain," Gwen said, "remember, this is a democratic environment."

"I have no objection to adding the item Varia to the agenda," Eugene said, "but I think we should set some ground rules about how this item is to be used and under what conditions motions are to be made."

"For example?" Kevin asked.

"For example, matters raised under this item should be for discussion only, while motions relating to these matters could be put forward only at a subsequent meeting," Eugene said.

"That sounds reasonable," Kevin said.

"Yes," Vivian agreed.

"So it's agreed, "Kevin said, "Varia will become a standing item on the Agenda?"

"It's agreed," Eugene said.

The item, Varia, was added to the Agenda and the Agenda was approved.

The next item was the Chairman's report. Seymour had attended yet another conference and went on at length about that.

The next item was The President's Report. "I am going to turn my report over to the Comptroller, who, as promised, has prepared a report on the surplus."

"Objection," Gwen said.

"Now what?" Réal said.

"In the December meeting a motion was passed instructing the Comptroller to submit his report to the Board. At the last meeting we were promised a report. I don't consider a verbal report as satisfying my motion. And, please, Eugene, do not say that the motion did not specify that the report be written. My motion specified that the report provide a detailed breakdown of expenditures."

"Gwen, if you hadn't jumped the gun you would have seen that you are getting just such a report," Paul said as he brought a sheaf of papers to the table and began passing them around.

"All this innuendo," Réal said, "over nothing, nothing."

"Why did we not get this report with the Board agenda, why is it being distributed only now?"

Shant asked.

"I don't believe this," Réal said, "nothing satisfies them, nothing."

"Mr. Chairman, can you please ask Réal to keep his comments to himself?" Shant said. "I ask the question again, why did we not get this report with the Agenda, why is it being distributed only now?"

"Because I only just got it ready in time for the meeting, Shant," Paul said. "This report took quite a bit of time to prepare and my department could not drop everything to work just on this.

You and all the other employees of the College do want your pay checks on time, I think, just as the Ministry expects its reports –"

"Mr. Chairman, I propose that we postpone discussion of this report until the next regular meeting," Walter said. "Immediately after the regular portion of this meeting we are going into a special session to hear our first briefs. I don't want a long, drawn-out discussion about this report to sap our energies."

"Right you are," Alain said. "I agree. Besides, this will give us time to study the report."

Seymour looked around the table.

"Since there is no motion on the floor," Michael said, "I think a show of hands would be sufficient to get a sense of how the members would like to proceed."

A show of hands was taken and the discussion was postponed until the next regular meeting.

Under the newly added item, Varia, Brendon gave notice of motion about Student Access to the Main Entrance for the next meeting, the regular meeting was adjourned and the visitors left the room.

"We will now begin the fifty-fifth special meeting of the Board of Directors of Penfield College," Seymour said.

Relax, Naomi told herself, breathe deeply and try to relax.

"As you know, we have received a total of twenty-five briefs from groups and individuals presently in the College," Seymour said. "We have also received two briefs from individuals who are no longer associated with the College. The motion regarding our procedures referred to briefs being solicited from members of the Penfield community. I have ruled that the briefs from the two individuals no longer associated with the College not be considered."

"Objection," Réal said, "I would like to know who those individuals are before rejecting what they have to say."

"Absolutely not," Shant raised his hand. "It is irrelevant who they are. If we had known that former members of the community could be heard, we could all have asked former employees or individuals associated with Penfield to submit briefs. These outsiders would not have known to submit briefs unless they were asked to. Who asked these individuals to submit briefs, that's what we need to know."

"If we are a democracy, then all opinions count," Alain said.

Oh, no, you don't, Naomi thought. She raised her hand. "But only citizens vote in an election," she said. "The question is who are Penfield's citizens. I am in agreement with the Chairman, only individuals currently in the employ of Penfield College, students currently enrolled at Penfield College and current members of the Board of Directors constitute the Penfield community."

"I agree," Brendon said.

"I don't agree, we may be depriving ourselves of valuable input. I think we should put this to a vote," Réal said. "That's what I move we do."

"I second the motion," Alain said.

"I have not had an answer to my question," Shant said. "Who asked these outsiders to submit briefs?"

"No one asked," Alain said, "People know what's going on - the two individuals stepped forward on their own and volunteered to do so."

"So again, you know something that we don't know," Shant said. "I wonder why that is? I repeat, these individuals are no longer associated with Penfield College and their views are not germane to our discussion."

"I call the question," Walter said.

Alain, Frederic, Irene, Louise, Philip, Réal and Walter voted in favour, Brendon, Carl, Dorothy, Gwen, Kevin, Michael, Naomi, Shant, Timothy and Vivian voted against, Jeremy abstained, Eugene and Seymour did not vote. The motion was defeated.

So Irene was on Eugene's side, Naomi thought glumly.

"I think it's a real pity," Réal said, 'I believe that one of the outsiders is a former Chairman of the Board."

"He wouldn't just happen to be the one who hired the President?" Shant asked. "What a wonderfully objective voice his would have been."

"He's out of order, Mr. Chairman," Réal said.

"As are you, Réal," Shant said. "In fact," Shant turned to Seymour, "I think we should solicit the input of all the administrators who have left Penfield in the past few years. I would like to hear their 'objective' opinions as well."

"He's out of order," Alain said.

"Uh - if we can get back to the matter at hand," Seymour said. "Of the twenty-five groups and individuals who have submitted briefs, fifteen have asked to speak to their submission. I propose that we consider the briefs in the order in which they were received, except for one, that of the Pedagogical Council, which, because the Council is most representative and has official status in the College, I believe we should hear last. I have invited five groups - representatives of four academic departments and the Support Staff – to be present this evening should the members agree to this proposal. This way we can begin our hearings immediately."

"I would have preferred organizing the groups by function, Mr. Chairman," Alain said, "for example, academic departments one evening, union groups another, administrative groups another."

Seymour looked around the table.

"I like the idea," Timothy said, "except the various representatives have been waiting all this time."

"Yes," Vivian said.

Seymour hesitated.

"Let us proceed this evening the way the Chairman has suggested," Kevin said, "and after this evening, the way Alain has suggested."

There was a murmur of agreement.

"May I also suggest a ten minute break before we continue, Mister Chairman," Kevin said. "I know it's going to be a long evening," he turned to Walter apologetically, "but I think we need to get a little air before we commence the important task ahead of us."

There was another murmur of agreement.

"Very well," Seymour said. "Ten minutes, then, everybody."

....

Interesting how the people were grouped, Naomi thought. Eugene, Alain, Réal, Walter, Irene and Louise constituted one group – yup, Irene was a lost cause. Kevin, Dorothy, Jeremy and Philip constituted another – if only Kevin could influence the other three. Gwen and Carl were a group unto themselves. Typical, Naomi thought. She had noticed during the light suppers served before the meetings that Gwen and Carl did not socialize much with the other Board members. Well, after her tête-à-tête with Gwen, she certainly had nothing to say to either Gwen or Carl.

Seymour, Timothy, Vivian, Shant and Brendon constituted the remaining group. That was interesting, too, that Vivian, teacher though she was, was not conversing with Gwen and Carl. But she had seen enough of Vivian to know that Vivian was not coming from the same place, that Vivian's concerns were much broader than theirs. Frederic and Michael had disappeared.

Naomi attached herself to Seymour's group. Vivian asked Seymour something about the last conference he had attended. That was a big mistake, Naomi thought, because Seymour now embarked on a long disquisition on the matter. Patience, Naomi enjoined herself, patience, she couldn't very well walk away, Seymour would be offended. She glanced at her watch – there were five minutes before the real drama began.

....

"I would like to introduce David Frye, Chairman of the English Department, and Emily Inman, Assistant Chairman," Seymour said after the Board members had regained their seats and David and Emily had taken their places around the table. "David, you may proceed."

"Good evening," David said. "Thank you for giving us the opportunity to address you this evening. I would like to begin by telling you a little about how this brief came about. When I brought up the idea of a brief at a Department meeting, there was unanimous agreement that we should write something. And when Emily and I wrote what you see and submitted it to all our members, there was unanimous support for what we had written. I believe it is important for you to know that the views expressed in this brief are not the views of two people sitting here but of every member of the English Department." David looked around the table. "Having said that –"

"If I may, David," Emily interjected, "it will surely interest the members of the Board to know that our Department is the biggest in the College – there are thirty-four of us – and although we get along well, we are rarely unanimous about anything."

"Right, Emily, thanks," David said. "We tried to keep our brief as short as possible – not so easy for English teachers to do –" David looked up from his notes and smiled, "and I will try not to take up too much of your time this evening either.

"As you have seen, we have one major concern, the concentration of power in the office of the President and the administrative and academic paralysis that has resulted from this. Everything that is right about the President – the stabilizing of Penfield's financial situation – is also what is wrong about the President.

"Everything costs money – curriculum research, curriculum change, administrative change – and since no one but the President has the right to approve any expenditures, nothing can move forward without his approval.

"But the process by which the President's approval is obtained remains mysterious. Requests that go through proper channels, that are approved by the Assistant Dean or the Dean himself, end up in limbo or are refused, while requests that have come out of the blue suddenly get approved.

"The result of the concentration of power in the office of the President and the President's use of this power in a non-consultative and secretive fashion has had a very negative effect on morale in the College. Departments that don't play the game – some refuse to play the game, some don't even know that there is a game – find themselves denied release time, denied space, denied funds for new proposals. This is not the way to run an educational institution. One man cannot know everything, and the result of one man's attempting to control everything has had a paralyzing effect on the academic life of the College.

"Furthermore, the President has also taken it upon himself to make all kinds of academic decisions that we think he is not qualified to make. The President's background is in business, not in academia, and his precipitous decision to offer non-credit English courses last summer – a decision taken without consulting either our Department or the Remedial specialist or the Admissions Office - was very badly thought out and would have been a disaster from a curricular and administrative viewpoint. We had to spend an inordinate amount of time and energy to fight an idea that, devised by someone who does not believe in consulting those who have the expertise, had no idea that his idea was totally unworkable at the time.

"Another decision taken without consultation was to open a Business Centre downtown. We question the location of the Centre or the need for the Centre – our Continuing Education Department could well have been given the responsibility for this enterprise and the money spent on paying expensive rent for office space downtown could better have been spent on hiring proper staff to develop the business training programs the President is so intent on.

"We have given other examples of questionable academic decision-making in our brief. Because of the time limit we have been given, I will not summarize them for you here but I would ask you to take note of them.

"The President prides himself on his administrative prowess, and, as you know, Penfield has two administrative committees, the Management Committee and the Academic Policy Committee.

But we would like to know why the President chairs both committees, why the Academic Dean does not chair the Academic Policy Committee, why the Academic Policy Committee has not been given some spending powers, why the recommendations of the Pedagogical Council, the most representative and most important consultative group in the College, a committee chaired by the Academic Dean and composed of faculty, professional, support staff and student representatives, are never heeded? The recommendations of this body in support of two of our long-standing and very popular mini-programs – Women's Studies and Black Studies – have been ignored, the recommendations about space allocation and about student concerns – including access by students to the main entrance - have been ignored.

"I have taught English at Penfield since its inception. Yes, there was more money available to the colleges when they were first founded than there is now. Yes, Penfield was not well-managed financially at the outset and Mr. Guzman has righted that situation. But to take a leaf from my colleagues in the History Department, we must not be like the generals who keep fighting the last war, we have to take a proper reading of the present and prepare adequately for future wars. I do not remember a time at Penfield when faculty was so demoralized, when tension was so high, when decision-making was so arbitrary." David turned to face Eugene, "I am not saying anything you haven't heard me say before, Eugene." David turned back to Seymour. "Mr. Guzman has not shown himself receptive to any of the criticisms leveled at him, to any of the appeals directed to him." David looked around the table. "Penfield needs a change in leadership, a change at the top. We urge you to make that change so that Penfield can renew and re-energize itself, something that we believe will not happen so long as Mr. Guzman remains in office. I thank you for your time."

"Thank you, David," Seymour said. He looked around the table. "Are there any questions?"

"I have a question about the Women's and Black Studies Programs," Kevin said. "Can you elaborate a little about what you were referring to, David?"

"Yes. The faculty of those mini-programs developed two new courses that Pedagogical Council approved unanimously. Both courses require small expenditures of money for materials and resources. Despite repeated requests, those funds have not been released."

"I see," Kevin said.

"Are there any more questions?" Seymour asked.

There weren't. The representatives of the French Department came in. They spoke briefly, reiterating some of the same points raised by the English Department. There were no questions and they left the room.

It was now the turn of the Business Administration Department. Seymour introduced Robert Taddeo, Gideon Farber and Jerome Van Gelder

"Thank you for giving us the opportunity to address you this evening," Robert said. "We assume that you have read what we wrote in our brief so we thought we would simply highlight our major points. Gideon, will you begin?"

"Thank you, Robert," Gideon said. "I would call your attention to our first point, what we have called accounting obfuscation. For all his purported financial prowess and despite all our repeated requests, the President has not provided departments with firm budgets and clear accounting records. Money that we think is ours to spend suddenly disappears from our budgets. Accounting records are not clear or reliable and departments have taken to keeping their own records, which seldom correspond to the records of the Accounting Department. This is no way to run a college that has twenty-seven academic departments.

"Further on this matter, this college has accumulated a surplus of approximately $700,000 in the past few years. When we asked how this money was being spent, we were told it was being spent on renovations. But other than small renovations here and there, we do not see anything that could possibly add up to $700,000. The Penfield community has a right to know how this money is being spent and how this money can be accessed. After all, this money is not the President's money, it is the College's money. Thank you."

"I'm next, I believe," Jerome said. He looked around the table. "Another one of our complaints is about space, there is a shortage of classroom space, resource room space, teacher office space and student space. Yet in the past two years administrative space has grown considerably at the expense of all of these. We don't expect the President to create space where there is none, we do expect the President to manage this precious resource with more concern for the mission of this institution, which is to facilitate the teaching and learning that is supposed to happen here. Thank you."

"This segues nicely into our last point," Robert said. "All of us have had experience in business, some of us as accountants, some of us as managers in both small businesses and large corporations, some of us as lawyers. Businesses do not survive without planning. Colleges may survive without planning but they are going to flounder badly. This College is floundering because there is no planning. The President refused to present his plans for the College when asked to do so by the Pedagogical Council last year and the year before that. He has refused to write anything resembling a mission statement for Penfield. You may ask, why do we need a mission statement? I'll tell you why, because a mission statement is like a course outline, it forces you to state your objectives and intentions clearly, it focuses your energies and attention, it allows you to measure your progress and your accomplishments, it permits transparency. All of this is lacking at Penfield, all of this is lacking in Mr. Guzman's leadership, and that is why we wrote our brief and have come here this evening to add our voices to those asking for a change in leadership at Penfield College. Thank you."

Thank you, gentlemen," Seymour said. Again he looked around the table. "Are there any questions?" he asked.

Kevin picked up his hand. "I am disturbed by your statement that departments are not given clear budgets and clear accounting reports. Can you elaborate on this?"

"We have a budget of $4,000 a year for printing, books, audio-visual materials, etc...," Gideon said. "Last year $450 was removed from our budget without our being told. When we discovered this, we were told that this was for audio-visual expenses. Spent by whom? Not by us.

Given to the audio-visual department because they had a shortfall? Maybe. But how can we be expected to administer our budget properly when the administration dips into it to help another department? At least that is what we assume happened."

"Thank you," Kevin said.

"Are there any other questions?"

"Yes," Naomi raised her hand. She wasn't nervous, she noted. That was because her question was totally impersonal, she realized. "Robert, I'm interested in what you said about a mission statement for Penfield. When did that come up? Who suggested it?"

"George Pappas, one of our colleagues who used to work for Bell Canada as a division supervisor, he's the one who suggested it. We thought it was a good idea and mentioned it to the Dean who said he would pass the suggestion along. We have heard nothing about it since."

"Thanks," Naomi said.

"Are there any more questions?" Seymour asked.

There weren't and the Science teachers were ushered in next. They too complained about poor accounting procedures, poor management of space and low morale. There were no questions, they left and the Support Staff representatives were ushered into the room.

Seymour introduced Pat Miranda, President, and Luc Rousseau, Vice-President of the Association.

"Thank you for giving us this opportunity to address you this evening," Pat began. "We have given you a history of our Association in our brief so I won't do that again tonight." She looked down at her notes and began to read from them. "The point we have come here to make this evening is that we are a union. To some people, that's a dirty word, union. We don't think it's a dirty word at all, we think the word merely sums up a situation, one that occurs when workers occupying similar positions unite to try to achieve good working conditions." She looked up briefly from her notes and then looked down at them again. "The means by which this is achieved is by written contract, and a contract works two ways, as you all know. It makes the workers abide by certain rules and it is supposed to make the employer abide by certain rules.

"Our problem with this administration," Pat continued to read from her notes, "with Mr. Guzman, because he heads the administration of Penfield College, is that the rules for hiring support staff, for replacing support staff who are on leave, for compensation to be paid for overtime worked, for sick leave, are not followed. What we consider clear and straightforward procedures according to the union contract, a contract that the administration has signed, have been ignored time and time again.

"We have given many examples of what we are talking about in our brief so I won't waste your time by repeating all that now. What I really wanted to say to you this evening," Pat looked up for an instant but looked right down again, "is that we are not uncooperative and unreasonable people, but our complaints, which do not date from yesterday, have consistently fallen on deaf ears. That is why we have decided to come forward, not without trepidation -" Pat's voice cracked and she had to stop to compose herself. When she resumed, her voice was barely audible, "- we have decided to come forward and voice our position against the renewal of the term of office of Eugene Guzman as president of Penfield College. Thank you."

The poor woman, Naomi thought, that took all her courage. She would have to call her in the morning and congratulate her.

Silence reigned in the Board Room.

She wasn't the only one absorbing Pat's drama, Naomi thought.

"Are there any questions?" Seymour asked finally.

There were no questions and the Support Staff representatives left the room.

Seymour looked around the table. "I now open the discussion," he said. "Does anyone have any comments?"

"Yes," Alain said, "I do. The President should be given the right of reply. Before any of us say anything, I think the President should be allowed to speak."

Seymour hesitated.

Eugene did not hesitate, stepping right in. "Thank you," he said, "I do have something to say. I heard all the presentations and, frankly, I don't recognize Penfield or myself in the things that people said. I know that my goals for this College are very clear. People have often heard me refer to Penfield as the Harvard of Quebec colleges. That's my goal, to maintain that, so it comes as a surprise to me to hear people criticize my administration for a lack of clarity about this.

"I am pleased that many of the representatives recognize that this College was in dire financial straights when I became President and that I have righted its financial situation. I never expected thanks for this, but I guess when you institute financial controls, you don't get thanks from the people whose budgets you oversee and sometimes restrict.

"As for the smaller complaints that people have, frankly, I don't understand why people haven't come to talk to me about them. My door is always open, I am always prepared to discuss any problem an individual or department might have. Some of the things people said here this evening, why, that's the first I ever heard of them. I can't solve problems if I don't know about them, can I?

"I also have a general comment to make and it's this. When you take any situation and have different people comment on it, you will always have different perceptions, different takes on what is really going on. That's what I feel is happening here, that there are different perceptions about what's going on here. It stands to reason that not all decisions an administration makes will be popular but we are not running a popularity contest here, sometimes administrators have to make tough decisions. With due respect to all the representatives, if a college administration waited for consensus on certain matters it would wait a long time or never make any decisions.

Furthermore, faculty and staff have their interests, but as an administrator our greatest obligation is to the government to act responsibly. That is what this administration has done. No one has mentioned the validation procedures we developed here at Penfield that the Ministry has since adopted province-wide. That's making a contribution to the collegial system, but I haven't heard one word about this. And that contribution has opened doors for us, believe me. It has meant that specific concerns we may have or specific projects we may wish to undertake get a sympathetic hearing at the Ministry. That's what I see as my job –"

"Hear, hear," Réal said.

Naomi raised her hand. She was still calm inside, she noted. "With due respect, Mr. Chairman, saying that Penfield College is the Harvard of Quebec colleges does not satisfy the need to plan, to set objectives, to develop a mission statement. Can Mr. Guzman please comment on the point raised by Robert Taddeo?"

"With pleasure, Naomi," Eugene said. "As I said before, I always felt that my goals for Penfield were clear. To me a mission statement would simply be an amplification of those goals. I am a man of few words," Eugene smiled, "and I have always felt that it was important to keep things brief. Not having a mission statement does not mean that my goals for Penfield are not clear and that they are not always in my mind."

"I hope that satisfies you," Réal addressed Naomi, "it certainly satisfies me."

"It doesn't satisfy me," Gwen said, "just like one sentence would not satisfy the requirements for a course outline. Is that what testing all applicants was about, Eugene, to make us look like Harvard? Well, we aren't Harvard, we are a publicly funded pre-university and professional college. A mission statement is not just a good idea, it's a necessity. And the elaboration of that statement is not something that should be left to the President alone, it is something that should involve the entire Penfield community."

"Hear, hear," Shant said.

"If I may be allowed to continue, Mr. Chairman," Eugene said, "I believe that actions speak louder than words. I admit that I have never believed in the utility of a mission statement, but if this Boards feels that this is something useful, why, we will certainly consider it."

"Mission statements are motherhood statements," Réal said, "I personally think they're a waste of time."

Kevin raised his hand. "Mission statements are what Mr. Taddeo said they were, Réal, a useful tool. I don't see how you can argue the opposite."

"I propose that we discuss this at future Board meeting," Walter said, "it's too late to discuss this now. I also propose that we adjourn."

....

Where was Timothy, Naomi thought on the way home, why didn't he speak up? They needed another outsider to help carry the ball, Kevin couldn't do it on his own. And she and Shant couldn't do what Timothy could do, sway Dorothy and Jeremy, maybe even another member or two.

She knew that Timothy was a very busy man and that he traveled extensively for his company. It was quite amazing that he was able to attend all the Board meetings, but they needed him to schmooze with Dorothy and Jeremy. They couldn't very well ask Kevin to do that, they might lose him. Had Seymour spoken to Timothy? Did Seymour and Timothy speak? And if Timothy didn't have time to schmooze with Dorothy and Jeremy, why didn't he contribute more during the meetings?

As for the meeting itself, she wished she had thought of it at the time, then again, maybe she wouldn't have had the courage to say it, although she hoped she would have - if, as you say, Eugene, actions speak louder than words, how can you dismiss all the complaints we just heard today as being due to a difference of perception? The people who spoke gave example after example of actions or lack thereof and said exactly what you are saying, actions speak louder than words. But she hadn't thought of it, and now it was too late.

Hopefully, there would be more opportunities. Above all what she had to remember to do was to step back and concentrate on the words of the man and think of how to throw them back in his face. The way she had done with Alain and democracy, that had been beautiful. The trouble was that the fear hardly ever left her belly and fear stopped her from thinking clearly.

No, fear just made it harder for her to think the way she had to think, for she still tended to think about the person who was speaking rather than about what they were saying, tended to see the motives and make-up behind a person's words and wanted to address that when in a public forum that was just not done. In a public forum you had to stay on the surface, you had to concentrate on the words.

Or, to put it another way, you had to be cool.

No, you could be hot, but controlled hot, à la Eugene and Alain and Réal. Not uncontrolled hot the way Timothy had been, or the way she had been in her interview.

The trouble was that she could not stop thinking about the motives and make-up of Eugene and his minions.

The trouble was that she could not help being an observer of human nature rather than a woman of action.

Maybe it had not been such a good idea to have her sit on the Board. It wasn't that she didn't have the courage to speak up, it was that she didn't think that quickly on her feet, that she was unable to distance herself sufficiently from the issue at hand – the desperate desire to get rid of Eugene - to deal with the words that were spoken rather than with what they masked, with the facts that existed rather than the spin Eugene put on them. That's why there were lawyers.

And Eugene had one on his side and they didn't.

CHAPTER 11

This time she had been a lot blunter, Naomi thought, yet she had still not managed to convince Dorothy.

It all came down to experience. She herself, history and political buff that she was, avid reader of newspapers and especially the current events page, steeped in the stories of the great dictators of her century as well as the lesser ones hence supposedly acquainted with evil, had still been stunned when Eugene had taken her job away. For in Eugene she had personally come up against evil for the first time – small-scale evil, but evil nevertheless - and contrary to what people thought, to what she had thought anyway, she saw that evil was not necessarily hot, as it was in those who hate, but that it was also cold, as in those who lust for power, and that in both types feelings for the other did not exist, there was no sense of a shared humanity, of commonality, otherwise the evil person would not behave the way he did.

Until she had seen this in Eugene, however – and the truth be told, she hadn't seen it, she had experienced it, because she still found it hard to believe whenever she looked at him, whenever she was in his presence. What went through the mind of someone like Eugene? What went through the hearts and minds of those who lusted for power? She could not fathom it. Was it a wonder Dorothy had trouble fathoming it?

"What do you think of the renewal process, so far?" she had asked Dorothy.

"I find it very interesting," Dorothy had replied, "but at the same time somewhat confusing."

"Confusing? In what way?"

"Well, you hear one thing and you decide one way and you hear another and you begin to wonder. Also, some of the people are a little too rough for my liking. Are all Boards this way?"

"I wouldn't know, I'm like you, I've never served on a Board before. I guess it would help if the Chairman imposed himself a little more."

"Honestly, there have been times when I was afraid Réal and Shant would come to blows."

"Réal brings it on himself, don't you think? We all know he's an unconditional supporter of Eugene, he has made that very clear, but he doesn't have to keep ramming his opinion down our throats all the time."

"I guess he feels strongly about this issue."

"Many of us feel strongly about this issue. But I believe that the strong feelings of some are more justified than the strong feelings of others."

"That's what's so hard for an outsider to figure out, whose strong feelings are the more justified."

"All you have to do is read, Dorothy, the briefs tell you everything."

"The briefs tell one side of the story, but as Mr. Guzman said the other night, he sees things differently."

"Dorothy, before I came to Penfield I taught high school at a small private school. I also spent one year as acting principal there. While I was principal I learned this, that when a few students complained about a teacher the complaints might or might not be justified, but when an entire class complained about a teacher there was something wrong with the teacher. Faculty and staff are unanimous, Mr. Guzman has become a disaster for Penfield from every viewpoint."

"That's not what his administrators said in their brief."

"What would you expect his administrators to say?"

"But that's my point, you have your viewpoint, they have theirs and I am just trying to find my way among all these viewpoints."

"Dorothy, think about this. Why would this wonderful administrator be so reluctant to discuss expenditures from surplus? Why would this wonderful administrator close the main entrance of the college to students? Why would this wonderful administrator disallow a Varia item on the Board agenda until forced to?"

"Yes, these are all good points, but it's hard to connect them to the Mr. Guzman I see during the Board meetings."

"Have you never met anyone before who talks a good line? Eugene himself said it, actions speak more loudly than words. The briefs are full of examples that make the same point again and again, the man does not listen, the man is secretive, the man is vindictive, the man is interested in only one thing, power, he is not interested in the good of Penfield College."

"I know you feel strongly about this, Naomi."

"I don't just feel strongly, Dorothy, I have tasted of the man's vindictiveness. You've read our Association's brief so you know that I had an 'incident' with Eugene. Well, let me tell you about this 'incident.' It happened because I balked at admitting the son of someone Eugene knew – a student much weaker than all the other students admitted to Penfield. Ultimately, though, I did admit the student but that wasn't enough for Eugene, he had to go after me. And while I was on leave he approached my replacement and asked that a hundred admission places be set aside for him to fill. This in a college that is publicly funded and by the man who says that his goal for Penfield is to make it the Harvard of Quebec colleges!"

"I hear you, Naomi, I hear you, and I like you and trust you, but I still have trouble connecting everything you are saying with the person I have seen at the Board meetings."

"Maybe this will help. If I didn't know all the things I know about Eugene, I would tend to believe him too, he talks such a good line. But it's his actions you have to attend to, not his words. Eugene does not use words in the way you and I use them, he'll say anything to defend himself, if he thinks it will work for him. What's more, he believes those words when he says them but that doesn't mean he is to be believed. You have probably never met anyone like this before. Until Eugene, I hadn't either." She had better stop, she had thought, she couldn't push Dorothy more than she already had. "But enough about all of this, tell me about your son, how is he doing in his courses?"

So Dorothy's life experience had not prepared her for a Eugene and she had not succeeded in getting through to Dorothy, in puncturing Dorothy's belief in words, in impressing upon Dorothy the total disconnect between Eugene's words and Eugene's deeds.

CHAPTER 12

It was happening again, Naomi thought. Even she felt it, she who had experienced the full lash of Eugene's spite and willfulness, who knew him to slither and slide this way and that around the truth. What was it that she had read about Simone de Beauvoir, brilliant anti-fascist intellectual that she had been, that when Petain had taken over as head of Vichy France, de Beauvoir had actually felt a sense of relief and hope, as if people, even the most aware, most politically astute people, could not help wanting to believe in the possibility of accommodation and reconciliation.

And if she felt it, how could Dorothy not feel it, how could Dorothy not be lulled and gulled by it?

Four faculty departments and two faculty members had presented their briefs this evening. Their complaints were the same as those of the departments that had preceded them. There was no consultation, there was no planning, teachers were treated badly, the space situation had deteriorated, the budget situation was intolerable, decisions were taken unilaterally and incredible energy had to be spent undoing what should never have been decided or undertaken in the first place.

Some representatives spoke better than others – it was a source of puzzlement to Naomi that some teachers could speak as badly as they did, that they made no attempt to project their voices or look up from their texts to make eye contact with Board members – but the messages had been identical, only the proofs varied, with some examples being ones they had heard before and others being new and specific to the departments concerned.

There had been a few questions here and there, but generally, the briefs had been received politely and quietly.

Then the last presenters had left the room. And the doors of the Boardroom had closed and the atmosphere inside the room – a large, windowless room - had undergone a complete change.

For with the closing of the doors - those imposing mahogany double doors that extended from the floor almost to the ceiling - the outside world had ceased to exist, only the small, inner world of the Boardroom remained, an inner world composed of nineteen individuals gathered around the table to deliberate the fate of the twentieth individual sitting amongst them, Eugene Guzman.

A Eugene Guzman who repeated his performance of the previous week with the same brio. He had been misunderstood, he had been maligned, if only people had come to him, he didn't understand why people didn't come to him, his door was always open, he was always ready to listen to what people had to say. He didn't know where all those perceptions had come from, if he had known sooner he would have tried to mitigate them, although he made no bones about the fact that as a responsible administrator he had to act even if people might not always like what he did, because that was his job, to listen but also to act, to make decisions, he could not always wait for the results of a consultation, sometimes speed was of the essence, and if his sin was that he sometimes made decisions that others did not approve of, why, then, he admitted it, he was guilty…

And so on and so forth.

The room was warm, it was comfortable, Naomi could feel people being lulled by Eugene's words. She would have been too, she was pretty sure, if she hadn't had the experience she had had - people wanted to believe that all was well, that the person sitting before them was not malign and willful, that he was as pleasant, reasonable and well-meaning as he presented himself to be. All the criticisms that had seemed so deadly five, ten minutes earlier had lost their sting, had paled into insignificance, had melted away, having been borne off by the visitors when they had left the room. A living, breathing individual sat before them denying it all, insisting he had been misunderstood, asking that he be given the benefit of the doubt...

The whole set-up was a mistake, Naomi thought, but it was too late to do anything about it. Eugene was having the last word whereas there should have been a debate between the presenters and Eugene, not these two solo dances with the presenters going through their routine and Eugene going through his without having to answer to any of the specific points raised by the first.

And the man was clever, you had to give it to him. When there was a factual mistake in anything that had been said, he pounced on it, and even though the mistake might have been a tiny, technical one, pointing it out tended to defuse the criticism that had come with it. Of course, when there was no mistake and the criticism had been devastating, he simply did not address the issue, defusing it by the simplest of methods, eschewal.

She would have to warn Andrew who would be presenting their Association's brief next week. They had to try to blunt the strategy that Eugene was employing...

Chapter 13

" I would like to present Andrew Roper, President of the Association of Penfield College Professionals, and Ricardo Johnson, Vice-President of the Association," Seymour said. "I understand that Mr. Roper will be making the presentation."

"Yes, Mr. Chairman, thank you." Andrew looked around the table. "Good evening, everyone, thank you for giving me the opportunity to speak to you this evening.

"I would like to begin by telling you that our original brief was twenty- five pages long. As a psychologist whose goal is to improve the emotional and mental health of my clients, I knew that I would be contravening the code of ethics of my profession if we inflicted that number of pages on you." There was a ripple of laughter around the table. "My colleagues agreed and so we cut our brief down to the ten pages you received.

"But," Andrew took the time to glance around the table and look some of the members in the eye, "we did have twenty-five pages, twenty-five pages that gave even more examples of the kind of mismanagement we have been subjected to, the kind of illogic and arbitrariness that characterize the administration of the incumbent president of Penfield College, Mr. Eugene Guzman.

"Have I just shocked you – I meant to shock you, to make you sit up and listen, to help lift the words off the pages we have written and fix them in your minds and lodge them in your understanding." Andrew paused while he rearranged his notes.

"We have presented you with all kinds of examples of mismanagement and arbitrariness," Andrew resumed, "but of all the examples we have given you, two stand out. One is the outrageous treatment meted out to Naomi Singer, who sits amongst you, whose capabilities and professionalism you have had the opportunity to observe with your own eyes, who was granted a discretionary pay increase by the College and by Eugene Guzman while she was on leave. A discretionary pay increase, Ladies and Gentlemen," Andrew looked around the table again, making sure to again lock eyes with some members, "meaning there was no obligation on the part of the College to grant this increase, meaning that Naomi was one of only a few people thus recognized." Andrew paused to let his words sink in. "Naomi was stripped of her job when she came back from her leave without so much as a word of explanation being given to her as to why this was being done.

"I suggest to you, Ladies and Gentlemen of the Board, that it is your job to get this question answered.

"The other example we have of mismanagement and arbitrariness is the passing over for promotion of an exceptionally qualified individual, Alison Browne, for the position of Registrar.

Alison has done it all, scheduling, advising, registration. Alison was also granted a discretionary pay increase a year ago. Why was Alison not hired for the position when the hiring committee recommended her for it? Why was someone without any experience at all hired for this position?

"This is another question that you should get answered." Andrew paused to take a sip of water.

"I can just hear what you are thinking, partial, he is partial and we had better take everything he says with a grain of salt.

"I have three things to say about that. First, what we have presented to you in our brief are facts, and facts cannot be partial, facts are facts.

"Second, we are all human, therefore, from that viewpoint, we are all partial, the President included," and here Andrew looked Eugene straight in the eye, "so partial is not a reproach."

She had known Andrew had guts, Naomi thought, but he was being amazing.

"Third, having said all that, guess what, I admit to being partial, partial to the truth, partial to justice, partial to what is right and good. And what I and my colleagues see happening at Penfield is the opposite of right and good, it is arbitrary and willful, it is bad and wrong.

"That's what I've come to say to you. Please read what we have written, please remember what I have said, please act the way we are asking you to act. For the sake of Penfield College, please, please, do not renew the mandate of Eugene Guzman as President of Penfield College."

She should have been the one to challenge Eugene after Andrew left, Myra thought, she should have been the one to ask him point blank why he had done what he had done, why had he paid another person to do what she should have been doing while he made her wile away her time on make-do projects? So much for fiscal responsibility, she could have added, looking at Alain and Real directly. And as a final question she could have asked, did the money just happen to come from the surplus?

But she had not had the guts. Her voice would have shaken, she was sure of it, if fear had not tightened her vocal chords to the point of inaudibility. Or, worse, she was afraid she would start to cry. Andrew should have been their representative, he was like Shant, not afraid to confront. She was a coward and had failed her own cause. Her case became one more item among many Eugene had simply eschewed.

. . . .

Now, Naomi thought after the Teachers' Union had presented their brief – a tepid brief, one in which the Union did not make a recommendation either way, so Lynne had been right, Carl and Gwen were going to split their vote - the Administrators theirs and the Pedagogical Council theirs, take the bull by the horns and ask the question, why did you do it, Eugene, tell us all, why did you do it?

But she didn't have the stomach for it, she knew what Eugene would say, he would utter the same gibberish he had uttered in her meeting with him, she would then have to debate him point by point and she still would not be able to throw the name of his grace-and-favor student in his face because she had no proof that that was why Eugene had gone after her the way he had.

It had not been a good idea to have her sit on the Board, Andrew would have been much better at it. She might not have been there to give living proof of her capabilities, but Andrew would have been better at going toe to toe with Eugene - à la Shant - and confronting him every step of the way. Unfortunately, she had neither the inclination for this nor the ability.

CHAPTER 14

How had he known, Naomi kept wondering on the way home from the Board meeting, how had Eugene known? He hadn't hesitated for an instant, he had been on his feet in a thrice. "An abstention," he had cried, "the motion was defeated by an abstention. My god, that's unfair, surely everyone can see the unfairness of that, I would accept the verdict of the Board, but to lose on an abstention..." and he had bounded around the room. "Surely you can see the unfairness of that," he had stopped before Irene. "A second vote," he had stopped before Jeremy, "I want a second vote," he had stopped before Dorothy, "I want a second vote, a clear vote," he had demanded.

How had Eugene known not to attack Seymour nor the legality of the vote - for neither would have worked - but to alight on the one soft spot in the process, the spot that had some give, and to pitch his plea to the three quietest people on the Board, one of whom had to be the abstainer – Irene, Jeremy or Dorothy.

Alain had immediately obliged. "I move that we revote," he had said. "I second the motion," Réal had said, and she had known then and there that they were going to lose. Because the abstainer had to have been Dorothy – come to think of it, Eugene must have known too, he would have figured out just as she had that Irene and Jeremy were his – and Dorothy, who had stayed neutral until the end, was not going to be able to stay neutral in the face of Eugene's appeal, that confronted with the fact that she, and she alone, now had the power to renew him or remove him – no one else was going to change their vote – she would not be able to bring herself to do the latter.

Many factors had brought the Board to this pass. There was Seymour's ineptness and his inability to rally to the cause the one or two people who might have been rallied, perhaps Irene, certainly Jeremy. There was Timothy's lack of leadership - where had Timothy been when Alain and, particularly, Réal, had bullied them all? There was Alain's strength - there was no denying it, Alain had been a most effective asset on Eugene's side. There was the Teachers' Union's treachery - there had been no convincing them, she had tried, she didn't know whether anyone else had tried to convince them, but Gwen and Carl had split their vote, they had to have split their vote, otherwise their side would have won outright. And, of course, there was her own lack of forcefulness for never having confronted Eugene about her case, for never having played the Steven Belair card during the surplus debate, but she had been incapable of doing so, incapable. Then again, if she had, would it have helped? But all of that was moot now, for everything had now come down to the two remaining factors, Dorothy's naiveté – here, again, Seymour's ineptness and Timothy's passivity had hurt, because either one might have succeeded in getting Dorothy onside – and Eugene's mastery of the word-spin, his ability to dress up subjective ends in objective garb, for it wasn't that Seymour had voted against him, oh no, it was that there had been an abstention, it wasn't that his personal desires had been thwarted, oh no, it was that someone had not voted and Seymour, as Chairman, in order to break the ensuing tie, had voted twice. Of course, had Seymour broken the tie and voted in his favor, Eugene would have stayed demurely in his seat and not said a word. And had anyone then proposed a revote on the grounds that Eugene's reappointment had been so weakly confirmed, they would have been roundly shouted down by Eugene, with Alain's and Réal's most vociferous assistance.

She had to hand it to him, Eugene and Eugene alone had pulled it out of the hat. He had found the one peg on which to hang his appeal and had gotten a second vote, the debate for which had been as predictable as the debate that had preceded the first vote.

Yes, the first debate had been predictable, but it had been good, nevertheless, despite Réal's contemptible editorializing. Of course, the debate had convinced no one, had changed no one's mind. For everyone who had come into the Board room that evening, into that inner sanctum, had made up their mind beforehand, even the one person who had not been able to make up her mind – except, unfortunately, she had not been able to stick to it.

Alain had opened the discussion by making a motion that Eugene's term of office be renewed.

Dorothy had showed her inexperience, when, after Réal had seconded the motion, she had exclaimed, "But…"

Seymour had turned to her. "Yes?" He had encouraged her to continue.

"I – I thought we were going to have a discussion first," Dorothy had said.

Seymour, showing his usual ineptness, had hesitated.

Michael had had to step in. "A motion on the floor does not preclude a discussion. It simply structures the discussion. You can speak to the motion or against it."

"Right. And I would like to speak to the motion," Alain had said. "We have heard a litany of complaints here for the past few weeks that, frankly, have disappointed me. Not one internal group or individual was able to step outside their small ken to speak to the larger picture, to acknowledge the contributions the President has made to Penfield College or the difficulty anyone in the position of president faces when trying to administer a college in an environment where the teachers are unionized, where the staff is unionized, where every step taken by the administration is constrained by petty rules and obstacles."

Naomi wrote down the word 'petty' on the note paper in front of her. She was not going to let Alain get away with that remark.

"Rather than criticize the President," Alain had continued, "the staff should have praised him for his accomplishments. I wonder whether any of the presenters know to what extent financial mismanagement is a problem in the public sector, to what extent there is a dearth of administrators with business expertise willing to step forward to bring to their positions the kind of pragmatism and realism Mr. Guzman brings to Penfield?

"But no, all we heard was endless criticism and carping. To an outsider like me, it was amazing to hear so much negativism. Frankly, when Mr. Guzman's term of office is renewed – because his term of office will be renewed, I have no doubt about that – I would advise him to address this negativism. In fact, the one small criticism I would utter about Mr. Guzman is that he has to do a better job communicating with all the constituents of Penfield College and informing them about what he is trying to do and how well he is doing it."

"If I may, Alain," Réal had raised his hand to speak.

"Yes, Réal," Seymour had recognized him.

"I haven't quite finished, Réal," Alain had said, "and I may have more to say later, but I wanted to reiterate what to me is the most important thing. My fellow Board members must gauge carefully who is doing the criticizing and why they are doing so, they must ask themselves what motives lie behind the torrent of negativism they have heard, a torrent belied by the facts and by the accomplishments of Mr. Guzman."

"I couldn't agree with you more, Alain," Réal had said, continuing in the same vein. "That's all we have heard, negativism and carping. I'm more excitable than you, I'm afraid, and I wasn't amazed by what I heard, I was angered and disgusted. I don't know how the President continues to function as well as he does in such a negative environment, but clearly he must be allowed to continue to administer Penfield College despite everything we have heard because, the way I see it, he must be doing something right if all these people with axes to grind are against him. These people must have been sharpening their axes for a long time to have treated us to the kind of spectacle we have witnessed.

"Shameful, it's shameful that anyone in Mr. Guzman's position should be subjected to this kind of mistreatment, shameful," Réal had concluded. "There, I've said what I have to say," he had added.

Vivian had raised her hand. "Have Alain and Réal been sitting in the same room I've been sitting in these past few weeks," she had begun, "have they heard the same things I have heard? I can only assume they must have difficulty hearing if they can dismiss everything we heard as a torrent of negativism. A flood of despair is what I would call it – same phenomenon," Vivian had paused to look around the table, "but with a correct interpretation this time. What must we do to demonstrate our deep concern about the future of this College, about the lack of consultation and communication, about the absence of clearly articulated goals around which people can mobilize and come together? I call upon every Board member to remember the briefs and letters they received. The groups and individuals who wrote to us and came to speak to us are pleading for change, are pleading with us to be as concerned about Penfield as they are. You must not dismiss what they have said, on the contrary, you must heed them. The future of Penfield is in your hands, my fellow members, and if you love this College as much as I do, you will heed them."

Naomi had raised her hand. Vivian had shown her what line to take, but first she would settle with Alain. "I would like to ask Alain a question. I would like to know why the union rules that regulate working conditions between the College and its employees are called petty while the government rule that allows the President to participate in a discussion about his own future – a most unusual rule even he would have to admit - is called a right – because that is what Alain called the rule allowing Mr. Guzman to participate in these discussions two months ago, a right. If Mr. Guzman is allowed his rights, so must employees be allowed their rights. I would appreciate Alain's not denigrating our rights by calling them petty.

"Then there is the charge of negativism that has been laid against those who have questioned Mr. Guzman's leadership. Vivian has responded to this charge most eloquently but I would like to add this. If those of us who find fault with Mr. Guzman's administration are negative, it is just as fair to characterize those who refuse to acknowledge the flaws in his administration as people who bury their heads in the sand."

"Right on, Naomi," Shant had said. "And what about that nonsense about axes to grind? The more complaints there are, the more Alain and Réal dismiss them. Logic dictates the reverse, I would have thought. Emily Inman said something very interesting when she was here on behalf of the English Department, that the Department is rarely unanimous about anything yet the Department endorsed its report unanimously. This College is made up of many different groups and individuals and they are rarely unanimous about anything. That so many groups and individuals took the time to participate in this exercise and that these groups and individuals are almost unanimous in their negative recommendations proves the depth and breadth of the problems we face.

"And before anyone points out that the administrators made a submission in favor of their boss, I would ask whether we should have expected anything different from Mr. Guzman's subordinates. If what faculty and staff say can be dismissed as coming from people who have axes to grind, then what administrators say can be dismissed as coming from people who dare not grind the axes they may have."

"Wait a minute," Réal had said, "you can't dismiss what the administrators said, they are the ones who work most closely with the President, they are the ones who know him best."

"Oh, come on, Réal," Shant had said, "they are dependent on him for their jobs. Whatever they say is biased."

"Funny you should say that," Alain said, "because that's exactly what I think you are - biased against Mr. Guzman because he is your boss, because he is decisive, because he dares to make unpopular decisions, because he has the toughness to stand up and be counted."

Naomi had raised her hand again. She wasn't usually very good at this kind of thing, but Alain and Réal made it easy. "That's funny, when Shant speaks against Mr. Guzman, Alain dismisses his comments as bias against his boss. When the administrators praise Mr. Guzman, Réal commends their comments as coming from people who know what they are talking about because he is their boss. Gentlemen, you can't have it both ways."

"Mr. Chairman," Timothy had finally intervened in the discussion, "accusations of bias are not going to get us anywhere. Let's face it, we are all biased if having an opinion means being biased. The representative of the Professional Association raised the same issue when he addressed us and refuted it very eloquently. The important thing, it seems to me, is for all of us to remember what people wrote and said and to weigh that against what Mr. Guzman says and then to make as informed a judgment as we can.

"Personally, I could not help but be impressed by the various presentations we heard," Timothy had continued. "I find that serious concerns were raised by many of the participants in this discussion and that as members of the Board, if we want to do our duty, we must consider theses opinions in our deliberations."

"I agree with what you said about bias, Timothy," Vivian had said, "but something else is going on here. Naomi put her finger on it a few minutes ago but it bears repeating. According to the way Alain and Réal would have it, whatever internal members say must be discounted because they are internal members. A dichotomy has been set up here that is totally false, implying that external members can be objective and clear-headed but internal members cannot be. That's like saying that the victims of a wrong cannot be counted upon to give an accurate account of their experience because they are victims. Who best can tell us –"

"Wait a minute," Réal had jumped in, "don't you dare talk to us about victims and wrongs –"

"Mr. Chairman, Réal is out of order," Vivian had said.

"Réal –" Seymour had said.

"Mr. Chairman, I cannot sit here and listen to this kind of calumny," Réal had continued.

"Mr. Chairman," Vivian had repeated, "Réal is out of order."

"Réal, you are out of order," Seymour had finally intervened, "Vivian, please continue."

"Disgraceful, that's what these shenanigans, are, disgraceful," Réal had said.

"Perhaps my words were not well-chosen, Mr. Chairman," Vivian had continued calmly, "let me amend them."

What composure, Naomi had thought, what a lady.

"To deny the participants of a situation the right to comment on their situation," Vivian had continued, "is to deny the people who best know their situation the right to bear witness. As Shant said, that doesn't make sense. Yes, people may have personal axes to grind, but like members of a jury, our job is to judge the facts for what they are, not to dismiss the things people say on the basis of who said them. Besides, if we follow Alain's and Réal's logic, we must dismiss everything Mr. Guzman has said since not only is he an internal member, he has more riding on this process than anyone, therefore he has to be the most biased of all."

And Eugene had jumped in here. "I agree with what you said, Vivian, I do have a lot riding on this process, but that's because I want to continue to contribute to the growth and flourishing of this College, to see it become even more of a model of achievement than it already is. And the only way to do that is for everyone to pull together, for everyone to make their contribution.

Unfortunately, that doesn't mean that everyone's opinion can always be taken into consideration and that's where things get a little tricky at times, because we all know that people do not always agree, they do not always have the same ideas about how to go about accomplishing certain goals. Well, one of the important components of my job is to judge between these different conflicting opinions and to decide. Naturally, any decision I take will displease someone, but that's what being president is all about, it's about making decisions, sometimes unpopular decisions, but just like you have to be true to yourself, Vivian, just like Gwen and Carl and Naomi and Shant have to be true to themselves, so do I have to be true to myself."

"Well said," Réal had said, "well and generously said."

"Thank you, Réal," Eugene had said.

And Alain had called the question.

And once again, Eugene had had the last word, Naomi had thought, once again he had made nice, a nice that was totally belied by his actions, actions that, before she had become a member of the Board, she would have thought were clear and irrefutable but that these many months of discussion and argument had shown her were only clear and irrefutable to those who wanted to see.

Michael had distributed the ballots and had collected them. He had then left the Boardroom with Brendon and Louise whom he had appointed as scrutineers and had gone off with them to a small office nearby.

Her mouth had gone dry, Naomi remembered, and her jaw had clamped shut tightly. She wanted so badly for Eugene to be ousted, wanted it so badly.

Michael had come back a few minutes later. He had whispered something to Seymour, who had gotten up and followed Michael out of the room.

A few minutes later Michael and Seymour and Brendon and Louise had come back into the room and had taken their seats.

Seymour had looked up. "My fellow Board members, the votes have been counted and a decision has been reached. The motion has been defeated."

"What was the count?" Alain had asked.

"As I said, the votes have been counted and the motion has been defeated," Seymour had said.

"What was the count?" Alain had asked again, "we have the right to know the count."

Michael had leaned over and whispered in Seymour's ear.

"The count was nine in favor, nine against, and one abstention," Seymour had said, his voice very low.

"That makes it a tie," Alain had said.

"The Chairman, in such an instance, has the right to break the tie," Seymour had said. His voice almost inaudible now, he had added, "And I broke the tie."

And that was when Eugene had jumped to his feet oh, so swiftly and had played his abstention card oh, so deftly, and Alain and Réal had obliged by making their motion to renew.

"Wait a minute," Timothy has said.

"There's a motion on the floor," Michael had said.

Naomi's heart had sunk. Eugene was going to get a second vote and Dorothy was not going to be able to maintain her neutrality in the face of Eugene's appeal, she was going to extend sympathy to someone, who – Dorothy's inexperience simply did not allow her to conceive it - would never have reciprocated in kind.

"I speak against the motion, then," Timothy had said, "the vote was fair and square and the motion was defeated. I move that we adjourn."

"A second motion cannot be made until the motion on the floor has been voted on," Michael had said.

"So what you're saying is that we have no choice but to vote on whether to re-vote," Timothy had asked.

"Yes," Michael had replied.

After a very brief debate – basically Timothy and Shant versus Alain and Réal, for she had not bothered to participate, neither had Vivian, as for Gwen and Carl, whatever they said had been as mealy-mouthed as their votes - the motion to re-vote had passed by a count of ten to nine. The actual re-vote had then also passed by the same count, ten to nine. In the final contest between Eugene and Dorothy – what was she saying, there had never been a contest - the results of the vote to re-vote and the re-vote itself had been a given.

Of course, had the initial verdict been in Eugene's favor, Alain and Réal would never have tolerated a re-vote. During the final debate she had tried to think of the arguments they would have used but had not been able to. Clearly, a re-vote was not illegal, since Michael had allowed it. At the end, Alain had had his democracy. Whatever the Board had decided, they could decide to decide otherwise a moment later.

Only at Penfield could these things happen, Naomi thought, only with a Eugene at the helm could things like this happen. Unfair, a clear, legal verdict had been called unfair.

Unfair – children used language like that, the applicants she dealt with sometimes used language like that, she had never heard a grown man use language like that. But it had worked because Alain and Réal had known what to do, because Dorothy had not been able to resist Eugene's appeal, because, because, because...

Because right did not always win, because justice was not always rendered, because, in the end, Eugene had proved himself a master of the word game. Like history with its immediate causes versus its underlying causes, many underlying factors had contributed to Eugene's victory, but there was no denying the last, immediate cause that had enabled him to achieve victory, the incredible nimbleness with which he had alighted on the one argument that could save his skin.

Eugene was a bastard, Naomi thought, she hadn't changed her mind for an instant, but, she had to admit, he was a wily bastard.

Yes, she thought ruefully, Eugene was one wily bastard.

EPILOGUE 1

A few days after the vote, Naomi met David Frye on campus.
"How are you?" David asked.

"I feel as if I have been through a war," Naomi replied. "I'm disappointed with the outcome, of course, but I'm very glad it's over."

"I'm optimistic, Naomi. Eugene won by only one vote. I can't believe he will not have learned a lesson from this."

"I wish I could agree with you, David, but I'm afraid I can't. Having watched the man operate, I feel pretty confident in saying that as far as Eugene is concerned, winning by one vote is the same as winning by a hundred votes. He is not going to change. As far as he is concerned, he won, and that's all that counts."

Naomi turned out to be right. After Seymour resigned from the Board – his position had become untenable – Alain was chosen as Chairman. While Alain was Chairman, a motion that Naomi and Brendon presented requesting that Eugene outline his future plans for Penfield was defeated. The surplus report – the spending guidelines that were listed in the report were so general they were meaningless – was accepted with hardly any discussion. A motion to buy the premises Penfield had rented downtown was presented to the Board without much prior notice and passed without a murmur. Needless to say, Eugene appropriated a lavish office for himself on these premises.

Naomi did learn that Alain's law firm had started doing business with Penfield College. Her Association sent a letter to the Minister of Education informing them of this. At the same time, they informed the Minister that the Board's Executive Committee had relegated to itself the power to spend up to $500,000 without having to seek the approval of the full Board. Within a week, Alain was unceremoniously dismissed from Penfield's Board. As well, instructions were received that the Executive Committee's spending limit was to be reduced to the province-wide norm of $25,000, that anything above that amount had to be submitted to the Board.

None of these changes affected the daily administration of the College. Nor did it stop the hemorrhaging of experienced and qualified staff. Michael and Charles – neither of whom had signed the Administrators' letter in support of Eugene – left Penfield. Lynne left, too, of course. Naomi looked for a suitable position elsewhere but could not find one, for, unlike Michael and Charles and Lynne, she was not willing to relocate to either Ottawa or Toronto.

It took Naomi over a year to get over her paranoia, for the fear to leave her whenever she came back to work after a day off, after a long weekend, after a vacation, the fear that something dreadful had happened while she was away. Only walking into her office and finding things as she had left them could dissipate her fear.

Naomi's relations with Stewart, the Registrar, were difficult. She found him stiff and without affect and couldn't help being on edge whenever she had to deal with him. After about a year of this edginess, she took matters into her own hands. She resolved to be herself with him, to allow herself to express her opinions, to make jokes – yes, jokes – and, suddenly, Stewart relaxed, too.

As for Eugene's grace-and-favor children, whenever Eugene 'inquired' about an unqualified candidate, Naomi admitted the student without balking but assuaged her conscience by admitting a worthy student who would otherwise have been refused because of lack of space, her reasoning being that if there was room for Eugene's student, there was room for one more worthy student as well.

While Stewart was Naomi's supervisor, he never made reference to their first encounter, to that sham interview in which he had participated. Stewart eventually changed positions, during which time Naomi's relations with him continued to be smooth and pleasant. It was only years later, when he was leaving Penfield and a small party was organized for him, that Stewart actually apologized to Naomi in public for his treatment of her. Naomi burst into tears. She could never think about that episode in her life, never talk about it, without bursting into tears. Even those many years later, the injustice she had been subjected to, the fear it had induced, the helplessness she had experienced, remained embedded in her bones.

EPILOGUE 2

Many more years later, and purely by accident, Naomi learned that the second vote on the motion to renew Eugene's term in office should not have been allowed. According to Robert's Rules of Order, a second vote on a motion that has just passed can only be moved by someone who has voted in favor of the motion. Since Seymour was the only person whose vote had been known and he had voted against, Alain's motion to revote had been out of order. Had Eugene known this? Had Alain? Michael hadn't known, neither had Seymour, and, obviously, neither had the others who had voted against Eugene, although Timothy had sensed it. But sensing had not been enough. She had faulted Seymour for his ignorance of Robert's Rules. It turned out that she and all the others who had voted against Eugene had been just as ignorant. And just as much at fault.

www.ingramcontent.com/pod-product-compliance
Lightning Source LLC
Chambersburg PA
CBHW021649120626
46545CB00002B/781